Advanced Critical Thinking Skills

Visit our How To website at www.howto.co.uk

At www.howto.co.uk you can engage in conversation with our authors – all of whom have 'been there and done that' in their specialist fields. You can get access to special offers and additional content but most importantly you will be able to engage with, and become a part of, a wide and growing community of people just like yourself.

At www.howto.co.uk you'll be able to talk and share tips with people who have similar interests and are facing similar challenges in their lives. People who, just like you, have the desire to change their lives for the better – be it through moving to a new country, starting a new business, growing their own vegetables, or writing a novel.

At www.howto.co.uk you'll find the support and encouragement you need to help make your aspirations a reality.

You can go direct to www.advanced-critical-thinking-skills.co.uk which is part of the main How To site.

How To Books strives to present authentic, inspiring, practical information in their books. Now, when you buy a title from **How To Books,** you get even more than just words on a page.

Advanced
Critical Thinking
Skills

Roy van den Brink-Budgen

howtobooks

In memory of my parents, who always encouraged me to aim as high as possible.

Published by How To Books Ltd
Spring Hill House, Spring Hill Road,
Begbroke, Oxford OX5 1RX
Tel: (01865) 375794 Fax: (01865) 379162
info@howtobooks.co.uk
www.howtobooks.co.uk

How To Books greatly reduce the carbon footprint of their books by sourcing their typesetting and printing in the UK.

British Library Cataloguing in Publication Data.
A catalogue record for this book is available from the British Library.

ISBN 978 1 84528 433 6

Cover design by Baseline Arts Ltd, Oxford
Produced for How To Books by Deer Park Productions, Tavistock
Typeset by PDQ Typesetting, Newcastle-under-Lyme, Staffordshire
Printed and bound by Bell & Bain Ltd, Glasgow

CONTENTS

PREFACE

My book *Critical Thinking for Students* introduces all of the central skills of the subject, so it makes a very good place to start if you want to develop these central skills. This more advanced book builds on those skills, taking us beyond analysis and evaluation of simple argumentation.

Any new title on Critical Thinking has to earn its keep in an increasingly crowded marketplace. This one does so in many ways. In addition to covering all the advanced skills needed for various assessments in the subject, it also provides a lot of material that can be applied to a wide variety of contexts. This will include organisations – both commercial and public – whose staff want (and perhaps need) to consider how Critical Thinking can help with decision making. Another feature of the book is that it uses plenty of international evidence (unlike many other texts from the US and the UK), thus making it of considerable value to a wide international readership.

Ultimately the book earns its keep by raising important questions about the central problem in Critical Thinking: the meaning and significance of claims. For example, it considers a problem that most texts don't even notice – what do we mean when we say a claim (evidence, especially) is 'relevant'? By using this questioning approach, the reader gets closer to answers. By getting closer to answers, we use Critical Thinking in a significantly productive way (rather than in a dull mechanical way that you might find elsewhere).

Much of the book has an obviously practical focus: how can a Critical Thinking approach clarify real claims and evaluate real inferences that are drawn from them? So the promise of the book is simple. It will enable you to attain high level skills in Critical Thinking for whatever purpose you need them for – passing an exam in the subject, making an organisational decision, putting together a highly persuasive presentation, asking significant questions about decisions or others' presentations, or whatever.

Of course, any book on Critical Thinking has to be willing to subject itself to such thinking. So, as Sir Francis Bacon said in his 1597 essay 'of studies', 'Read not to contradict, nor to believe, but to weigh and consider.' In the same essay, he explained that some books need to be 'chewed and digested' rather than merely 'tasted' or 'swallowed'. I hope that, in weighing and considering, you enjoy the chewing and digesting. Bon appetit.

1

THE STATUS OF CLAIMS
AND INFERENCES

Here's Ptolemy, a four-year-old boy, walking up the stairs with Celeste, his younger sister, and his father.

> *'I wonder who's going to get to the top of the stairs first,' Ptolemy says to his sister, Celeste.*

> *'You shouldn't run up the stairs,' Celeste tells him.*

> *'Yes, that's right, Ptolemy,' says his father. 'It's dangerous to race up the stairs.'*

> *'But I didn't say it was a race,' said Ptolemy. 'I just wondered who was going to get to the top of the stairs first.'*

Here we have a wonderful example of critical thinking in action. Both Celeste and Ptolemy's father took the initial point ('I wonder. . .') to mean that there was going to be a race. Perhaps there was: perhaps this is what was meant. But it didn't have to mean this. It could indeed have been just Ptolemy wondering who would be first, with no necessary implication.

What does this account illustrate? The very important point that, in Critical Thinking, we very often need to ask the questions 'What does this statement mean?' and 'What else could it mean?' Indeed, to be doing critical thinking is essentially to be asking lots of questions. Critical thinking without questions is like trying to listen to someone's conversation through a wall. You get bits of what's going on, but you miss important bits, such that all you get are disconnected words.

This chapter has three main purposes:

- To look at the issue of meaning and significance when considering claims;
- To examine how meaning and significance are central to what happens when inferences are drawn;
- To look at the relationship between claims and inferences drawn from them.

LOOKING FOR MEANING AND SIGNIFICANCE

We'll begin by looking at an evidence-claim in order to see the importance of considering meaning and significance.

The country that has won more Nobel Prizes than any other is the US.

It might seem that this is a straightforward evidence-claim, such that its significance is clear. But what is this significance?

Being top of any league table will tell us something about that which is the leader, so being top of the international league table for Nobel Prizes tells us something about the US (and about other countries too), but we might perhaps need to know more detail.

- How many prizes has the US won compared to other countries?
- Has the US won many prizes in some categories but few in others?
- Have some countries done even better when we look at population size?
- Were some of the people who won the US Nobel Prizes originally from other countries?

As you can see, asking questions about the claim can lead us to consider its significance better.

The first question is an important one. Is the US top of the league table, but followed very closely by the second-place country? If this were the case, then perhaps the significance is not as great as we might think. However, this isn't the case. The US is way ahead of all countries, having received almost three times as many awards as the country in second place. (The US had, by 2009, won 305 prizes; the UK, in second place, had won 106.)

The second question might be relevant if the US has achieved its high rank only by performing well in some categories. Nobel Prizes are awarded in the following categories: Chemistry, Physics, Medicine, Economics, Literature and Peace. The US beats every other country in all of these categories, except Literature where France comes top. (There is a category of winner which is labelled 'International' and which includes organisations like the Red Cross and the United Nations. If we include this category then the US doesn't top the poll for the Peace Prize, being pipped 22 to 20 by this international group. We would perhaps expect this 'International' category to be the leader of the Peace Prize, given the organisations it includes. The US remains, however, way ahead of any other country for the Peace Prize.) So the answer to the question is that they have won many prizes in all categories.

The question about population size is an interesting one. The current population of the US is 303 million. This would mean that there is an almost exact correspondence of one Nobel Prize per million of population (although this gives a somewhat artificial snapshot by comparing cumulative past performance with present population size). The current population of the UK is 60 million, which gives us an approximate figure of one Nobel Prize for every 600,000 people. The figure for a small country like Switzerland is even more striking. Its population is 7.3 million, which means its 22 awards give us an approximate figure of one per 330,000. At the other end we have China, with a population of 1,331.4 million and, so far, two prizes (both for Medicine). (But see below.)

So when we consider Nobel Prizes per head of population, then the figure for the US is not as significant as when we looked at the raw figures. If the Swiss performance had been matched by the US, they would have had 918 awards – although, of course, this would not be possible since not that many have been awarded.

The question about the country of origin of some of the US prize winners is also significant. For example, there are a number of US prize-winners who were originally Chinese citizens (as illustration, the two people who won the 1957 award for Physics were both originally Chinese).

So when we look again at the evidence claim:

The country that has won more Nobel Prizes than any other is the US,

we can now consider its significance with the benefit of greater information. This further information provides a wider and deeper context for the claim, encouraging us to refine any claimed significance for it.

The Swiss figures also give us scope for looking for significance. They would show that there isn't a necessary correlation between population size and Nobel awards.

Denmark provides another striking example of this: current population is 5.5 million and they've won 13 awards, giving a ratio of one award for every 423,000 people. A relevant question would be: 'Why have some countries won a disproportionately high number of Nobel Prizes in relation to their population size, while other countries have won none at all?'

So, if we were to look for the significance of the evidence-claim that the US dominates the league table for Nobel Prizes, we would have to ask the above questions and then more. If we draw an inference from this evidence-claim, then we have taken it to have a significance.

> The country that has won more Nobel Prizes than any other is the US. So the US education system must be the best in the world. / So the US puts more money into its leading universities than does any other country in the world. / So the US produces the most creative thinkers in the world. / And so on.

But, of course, this significance-giving requires that we have more information than just the claim. (The obvious point here is that without further evidence, we don't know enough about the topic.)

INFERENCE

We'll continue looking at how this questioning approach works by focusing on what is happening when a line of inference (or 'argument') is created. In other words, we'll look at the process by which significance is given to claims. The simplest line of inference would be when one claim is used to draw one inference.

> claim → inference

We look at this as a process in which the → sign is used to indicate, not just that there is a relationship between the claim and the inference, but that the relationship is one in a particular direction. The claim is used to draw the inference. (We could also use the word 'support'. There is one UK resource that uses the word 'causes', but this is quite simply, straightforwardly wrong.)

We'll take an evidence-claim and see how drawing an inference gives the claim a meaning.

> Children and young people spend many hours a day with various electronic devices.

The claim (a frequently reported one) is like other claims, in a very important way a neutral one. It merely states or reports information. It doesn't have a significance yet. It will have a significance only when someone does something with it. (It would be useful to look at my book *Critical Thinking for Students*, pp. 2–10, for an introduction to this link between claims, significance and inference.)

Here's an example.

> Children and young people spend many hours a day with various electronic devices. Therefore their studies at school and college will be disrupted.

In this example, the author takes the claim to have a particular meaning and, by the inference that is drawn, this meaning is given a significance. The author takes the claim to include the meaning that spending 'many hours a day with various electronic devices' will take children and young people away from their studies or will contribute to their not being able to adequately concentrate on their studies.

The claim in some way 'fits' with the inference: even if you don't agree with the inference, you can see that there is some scope for it. There is some connection that we can at least understand, whether or not we agree with it. But a different inference shows that a different meaning can be given to the claim.

> Children and young people spend many hours a day with various electronic devices. Therefore they are able to connect with a wide circle of friends and access many useful sources of information.

In this version, the claim is seen in positive terms.

CONNECTIVITY

This contrast between the two versions emphasises how the meaning given to a claim is central to how an inference gives the claim a significance. We judge this process of significance-giving in terms of what can be called 'connectivity'. In other words, to put it very simply, to what extent is the claim connected with the inference?

In the next version, there is a big problem with connectivity.

> Children and young people spend many hours a day with various electronic devices. Therefore children and young people are healthier than previous generations.

It is not at all obvious why there is any connection between the evidence and the inference. It might be that such a connection could be made but, until it is made explicit, the degree of connectivity is very low (even absent).

ASSUMPTIONS

This connectivity is very often the source of the missing parts of an argument. These missing parts are known as 'assumptions'. They are missing in the sense that they are literally not stated. Like an iceberg, most of an argument is often hidden. But an assumption is not just a statement or claim that's not stated: it's also essential for the argument to work. Look at this with the first inference that was drawn. As we considered above, the inference is drawn by giving a particular meaning to the claim.

> Children and young people spend many hours a day with various electronic devices. [*These electronic devices are not being used for their studies.*] [*'Many hours a day' refers to time spent on these devices that would otherwise be spent on their studies.*] Therefore their studies at school and college will be disrupted.

The two assumptions that are shown in this argument highlight how looking for them shows clearly what meaning an author has given the claim. These assumption-statements are indeed essential for the author's inference to be drawn. You will possibly know that the best way to check if a statement is indeed an assumption is to use the 'negative test': we simply turn the statement into its negative form and see how this negative version fits into the argument.[1] With the two statements above, you can see that the negative versions give a very different meaning to the initial claim.

> These electronic devices are being used for their studies.
> 'Many hours a day' does not refer to time spent on these devices that would otherwise be spent on their studies.

These negative (or, if you like, opposite) versions give an opposite meaning to the claim and thus would lead to an opposite inference. We can see this with using the first of the above negative versions.

> Children and young people spend many hours a day with various electronic devices. [*These electronic devices are being used for their studies.*] Therefore their studies at school and college will not be disrupted.

Using 'connectivity' to judge an inference, we can see that there needs to be a high degree of connectivity between the claim, the assumptions (or further claims) and the inference. We return to the issue of 'connectivity' in Chapter 4 where we develop it in relation to the issue of relevance.

LANGUAGE INTERPRETATION

Another aspect of this issue of a claim being given meaning is to focus on the author's interpretation of the language used in the claim. This issue of language interpretation is a very big one, and important for Critical Thinking. It is one that we examine in detail in Chapter 2 (and also look at in Chapter 3).

The obvious words that are problematic in the claim we have been looking at are 'many hours a day' and 'various electronic devices'.

- How many is 'many'? (Three, four, five...?)
- What sort of 'electronic devices'? (Computers, phones, MP3 players...)

But even the word 'spend' can be seen as problematic. The word can be seen in terms of time being given to the electronic devices perhaps to the exclusion of other activities or perhaps of time being shared between these devices and other activities (reading, taking exercise, and so on). Thus a young person could be reading something (perhaps connected with their studies) whilst listening to music on their iPod. Or they could be listening to a podcast on a topic to do with their course.

Of course, you will probably have seen that the word 'with' is also possibly problematic. It is taken to refer to 'using' rather than simply 'being next to/near' (as in 'I spent many hours with my brother.')

We have seen, then, that a claim (each part of it) is given meaning at the point that an inference is drawn from it. We have also seen that the 'connectivity' between a claim and an inference drawn from it requires that there is enough in the claim to provide the connection.

This is a central point whenever we're doing any Critical Thinking. By focusing on the possible meaning of a claim, we are looking at what limits there are (or might be) to any inference that could be drawn. At this point, it would be useful to have a preliminary consideration of what we mean by 'inference'.

THE MEANING OF INFERENCE

The question

> What is the nature of the relationship between claims and inferences from them?

is one that's often overlooked in Critical Thinking textbooks. Too often, the authors just start with talking about reasons and conclusions without troubling about the nature of the relationship between them.

So let's ask the question directly: What does 'inference' mean?

There are two main types of inference: inductive and deductive inference. (There is a third called 'abductive' inference, but it can be seen as a version of induction.) Most of the work that we do in Critical Thinking is inductive inference. We'll look at deductive inference later in this chapter.

INDUCTIVE INFERENCE

When we look at most arguments in Critical Thinking, we're looking at inductive arguments. In such arguments, the relationship between what's in the reason-side makes the conclusion at best probably rather than certainly true (or, we might prefer, that the conclusion 'is the case'). The process of inductive inference is one of extracting significance from the reason-side claim(s).

> Claim → it means this → so this follows.

When we use the words 'extracting significance', we mean that the arguer has given a significance to the claim(s) and taken that significance to give the inference. It would be more accurate therefore to describe inductive inference as 'the process of extracting imputed significance from a claim'. In other words, the person doing the inference takes the claim to have this significance (even though, crucially, others might not).

LOOKING AT THE PROCESS OF INDUCTIVE INFERENCE: THE PLIGHT OF THE ALBATROSS

Let's apply this discussion of inductive inference to an example and see how the process builds up step by step. Look at the next passage.

Each year 100,000 albatrosses are killed by fishing boats. The lines that boats use can stretch for 50 miles and the birds get caught in them whilst searching for fish for their young. Having got caught in the lines, the albatrosses are pulled under the water and drowned. Their chicks, sitting in nests possibly hundreds of miles away, waiting for their parents to return, die from starvation.

The passage consists of an evidence-claim in the first sentence. The second and third sentences give an explanation for the evidence-claim. The fourth sentence is a further evidence-claim.

Are these evidence-claims and the explanation sufficient for an inference? You will see that we're back to the point that a claim has a neutral significance until someone gives it a specific significance.

As ever, we need to ask questions.

- Is 100,000 a high number? In other words, is it a high proportion of all albatrosses?
- Does the 100,000 include both adult birds and their chicks or is the figure 100,000 plus chicks (an additional similar number or higher or lower)?
- Do other fishing methods cause higher or lower numbers of albatross deaths?

As you can see, these questions enable us to assess the claims for possible significance. But there are others. Here is a central one.

Are the deaths of albatrosses a problem – something to be regretted? After all, millions of birds die every week (chickens, ducks, wild birds and so on).

The answer to this question will produce another one.

If it is a problem, what sort of problem is it – a moral one, an environmental one, both of these?

This question, in turn, can be informed by asking a specific one.

Are albatrosses an endangered or vulnerable species?

You can see that, in looking at the possible significance of claims, asking relevant questions illuminates the claim. We can see its possible significance much more clearly.

Here are some answers to some of these questions.

● Of the 21 species of albatross, two are 'critically endangered' (with one – the Amsterdam albatross – having only 80 birds left). Seven are described as 'endangered'; ten are 'vulnerable'; two are 'near threatened'.

● One estimate of the total number of albatrosses of all species is three million. Thus the loss of 100,000 adult birds (for this is what the figure refers to) represents a loss of a thirtieth of the total albatross population each year (ignoring the variable impact of these losses on the species with already very low numbers).

● The longline fishing method is much more of a problem for the birds than other fishing methods, because of the length of the lines and how they work – by having baited hooks which attract the birds, causing them to get caught on the hooks and leading to fatal injury or drowning.

At this point, we can suggest an inference from the claims and the explanation because we've clarified the claims and extended the explanation.

> Each year 100,000 albatrosses are killed by fishing boats. The lines that boats use can stretch for 50 miles and the birds get caught in them whilst searching for fish for their young. Having got caught in the lines, the albatrosses are pulled under the water and drowned. Their chicks, sitting in nests possibly hundreds of miles away, waiting for their parents to return, will die from starvation. Therefore we should ban these fishing lines.

What can we say about this argument? There are two claims that are doing the work to enable the inference to be drawn (the first and the fourth sentences). In brutal summary, the argument is:

> 100,000 albatrosses die each year because of fishing lines + their chicks die → we should ban fishing lines.

This two claim-argument raises a very important question. Is an argument with more than one claim stronger than an argument that has only one?

So is the following argument weaker than the one we've been looking at?

> 100,000 albatrosses die each year because of fishing lines → we should ban fishing lines.

We'd probably say it is, but why? It's because when we're looking at the relationship between claims and the inferences drawn from them, there's the issue of balance. We always need to look at an argument in terms of its two sides. The more they are in balance, the better the argument is.

$$R \rightarrow C$$

This looks horribly unbalanced, like a featherweight boxer up against a heavyweight. Similarly, the following also looks very unbalanced.

$$R \rightarrow c$$

A big conclusion requires sufficiently big reasons (or just one sufficiently big one). Big reasons can support a big conclusion. This sums up the relationship between the two sides.

In one UK assessment of Critical Thinking, there is the belief that complex arguments are somehow better forms of argument than simple ones. Why this is so is never explained. The central point is that the quality of an argument needs to be judged not by complexity but by the balance between the reasons and the conclusion.

> 100,000 albatrosses die each year because of fishing lines → we should ban fishing lines.

This argument isn't without some useful degree of balance already. There's some power in the number 100,000. But banning fishing lines is a very big recommendation, so is it enough? This is where our questions help by providing greater significance to the reasons-side of the balance. But we'll first of all add in the deaths of the chicks.

> 100,000 albatrosses die each year because of fishing lines + their chicks die → we should ban fishing lines.

More deaths, so a stronger reasons-side. We can make it even stronger, by giving extra significance to the raw numbers.

> 100,000 albatrosses die each year because of fishing lines + this is equivalent to a thirtieth of the total albatross population each year + their chicks die + all of the species of albatross are threatened by longlining, with nine out of the 21 species either critically endangered or endangered → we should ban fishing lines.

The conclusion that we should ban longlining is still pretty big, perhaps too big for the reasons. So we need to keep adding in more on the reasons-side of the argument. After all, it might be argued that perhaps longlining isn't as big a problem as other types of fishing. But we know already that it is a very big problem, so let's use it.

> 100,000 albatrosses die each year because of fishing lines + their chicks die + all of the species of albatross are threatened by longlining, with nine out of the 21 species either critically endangered or endangered + the lines that boats use can stretch for 50 miles and the birds get caught in them whilst searching for fish for their young + having got caught in the lines, the albatrosses are pulled under the water and drowned → we should ban fishing lines.

Now the explanation serves as a reason that adds further weight to the reasons-side.

We might still be concerned that the conclusion is too big, too strong for our reasons. So in come further evidence-claims to make the reasons-side even stronger.

> The fishing lines that kill albatrosses also kill many other species of seabird. These include the critically endangered spectacled petrel (of which there are possibly only 2,500 left) and other species of petrel and species of shearwater.

> 100,000 albatrosses die each year because of fishing lines + their chicks die + all of the species of albatross are threatened by longlining, with nine out of the 21 species either critically endangered or endangered + the lines that boats use can stretch for 50 miles and the birds get caught in them whilst searching for fish for their young + having got caught in the lines, the albatrosses are pulled under the water and drowned + the fishing lines that kill albatrosses also kill many other species of seabird, including those that are critically endangered and endangered → we should ban fishing lines.

The reasons-side of the argument is getting stronger but is there something central to it that is missing? We know that longlining is a problem for albatrosses and other species of seabird. But is this problem something that should trouble us? There is a big assumption hovering around (albatross-like), shouting pretty loudly, alerting us to the question, 'So what that these birds are dying?'

The assumption is:

> The serious decline in the number of albatrosses and other seabirds is something to be regretted.

It might be thought that the more general assumption that 'the serious decline of any species is something to be regretted' is playing a part in the argument. But it is too general, too big. The argument is only about albatrosses (and other seabirds) and, though someone making it could well believe the general assumption, they don't have to in making this argument.

> 100,000 albatrosses die each year because of fishing lines + their chicks die + all of the species of albatross are threatened by longlining, with nine out of the 21 species either critically endangered or endangered + the lines that boats use can stretch for 50 miles and the birds get caught in them whilst searching for fish for their young + having got caught in the lines, the albatrosses are pulled under the water and drowned + the fishing lines that kill albatrosses also kill many other species of seabird, including those that are critically endangered and endangered + the serious decline in the number of albatrosses and other seabirds is something to be regretted → we should ban fishing lines.

COUNTER-REASONING

The argument keeps getting stronger as we load more into the reasons-side. Part of what's going on here is that we're closing off lines of possible counter-reasoning. For example, the inclusion of the evidence on other species of seabird closes off the possible line of counter-reasoning that, since other seabirds are not affected, the problem is not as bad as the author is making out.

But, with regard to counter-reasoning, the point could be raised that the interests of the owners of the fishing boats using longlining needs to be considered. Perhaps, it could be argued, the loss of seabirds is more than compensated for by the gain in fish caught. The argument does then have a hole that needs to be filled. One way would be to stress the inefficiency of longlining.

> Every time that a seabird gets caught up with the baited hook on the longlines is a loss to the fishing boat, as a result of the bait no longer being there to catch fish.

This point stresses that longlining can have a double loss: fewer fish caught and more seabirds killed. (Although, if you're arguing from the position of the fish, this is unconvincing.)

This is a difficult point to include in the argument itself. It would fit better as a counter-argument.

> Though it might be argued that the fishing industry should be allowed to get on with its job of catching fish, the use of longlining is inefficient as a result of seabirds attacking the baited hooks leading to a reduced catch...

ADDING TO THE STRENGTH OF THE ARGUMENT

To make the argument even stronger, we can move away from seabirds and look at other species affected by longlining, such as sea turtles. It is estimated that 40,000 are lost each year as a result of longlining. (Of course, we must extend our assumption with regard to regret to include other marine creatures.)

> Though it might be argued that the fishing industry should be allowed to get on with its job of catching fish, the use of longlining is inefficient as a result of seabirds attacking the baited hooks leading to a reduced catch. 100,000 albatrosses die each year because of fishing lines + their chicks die + all of the species of albatross are threatened by longlining, with nine out of the 21 species either critically endangered or endangered + the lines that boats use can stretch for 50 miles and the birds get caught in them whilst searching for fish for their young + having got caught in the lines, the albatrosses are pulled under the water and drowned + the fishing lines that kill albatrosses also kill many other species of seabird and other marine animals, including those that are critically endangered and endangered + the serious decline in the number of albatrosses and other seabirds and marine animals is something to be regretted→ we should ban fishing lines.

We could keep adding to the reasons-side of the argument.

> ... + the serious decline in the number of albatrosses and other seabirds and marine animals is something to be regretted + catching endangered species is illegal + longlining involves such illegality→ we should ban fishing lines.

You will remember that we referred earlier to connectivity in an argument. We can now see how it operates in increasing or reducing the strength of an argument. Lego bricks provide a useful analogy. The more connections the bricks have with each other, the stronger they are. On the other hand, if they have few connections, then they are weak and vulnerable to falling apart.

So we have, reason by reason, increased the connectivity of the reasons-side of the longlining argument to the inference/conclusion-side. But could we increase the connectivity in a different way?

Since the relationship between the two sides of an argument determines its connectivity or strength, we could look at either side to increase or reduce this. Thus, as well as increasing the reasons-side, we could reduce the inference-/conclusion-side. Continuing the Lego brick analogy, a reduced conclusion has fewer connecting points. Thus we can connect it more easily to a reasons-side that isn't comprehensive.

The conclusion of the above argument was this.

> We should ban fishing lines.

This has a wonderful simplicity to it. A position which says that there should be no x (or there should always be x) is easy to understand. (At one level, it is easy to operationalise, in that we would know what's to be done – even though we might not know how to do it.) The Chinese saying, 'simplicity is a blessing', captures all this very well.

FITTING THE REASONS TO THE INFERENCES

But the blessings of simplicity come at a price when we're looking at inference. For the inference on banning fishing lines to be drawn, we would need to address the problem that there are so many connectivity points to be responded to. We could therefore weaken it.

> The use of fishing lines should be greatly reduced.
> The use of fishing lines should be allowed only with adequate bird-scaring equipment.

In the first, the reasons-side can now connect with a smaller conclusion-side, asking for less from the reasons-side. In the second, the conclusion might work with regard to seabirds but it wouldn't deal with the point about other species such as sea turtles and sharks.

This whole discussion on the issue of strength of reasoning through connectivity has concentrated on trying to deal with the point that the degree of strength increases when more connections are made between the reasons-side and the conclusion-side.

We can approach this by looking at either the reasons-side or the conclusion-side. A useful way of approaching this from the conclusion-side is to think of the conclusion sitting there (Lego brick-like) with its connections waiting to be made. Thus, instead of starting with the reasons-side, we focus on the conclusion-side and consider what's needed to connect with it. Using this method, we could see that a conclusion might need very few reasons to be very strong.

We perhaps made life more difficult for ourselves by using an inference that was moral in nature. 'We should ban fishing lines' was a recommendation of what we ought to do. This was why we had to include the moral claim that the decline in the numbers of albatrosses was something to be regretted.

We could make life easier by drawing a non-moral inference but it might be difficult. Why should fishing lines be banned/reduced in usage unless we somehow regret the loss of species such as the albatross? It could be that we regret the disappearance of something as beautiful or impressive as the albatross but regret is still there. We could have seen the banning as concerned with stopping an inefficient way of fishing. (This was raised earlier when looking at the point about seabirds and other non-fish species being attracted to the bait, so reducing the number of fish caught.) However, we don't normally get involved in banning things simply because they're less efficient than others!

All of the above discussion has focused on the issue of the relationship between the reasons-side and the conclusion-side of arguments in what are called inductive arguments. In these, as we have seen, the conclusion is drawn from the reason(s), but is *not a required consequence* of the reason(s). This is an important point. The conclusion of the fishing line argument could have been different and any of the following conclusions could have been drawn instead.

- So fishing lines should be phased out.

- So some species of albatrosses could be extinct soon.

- So research needs to be carried out to reduce the impact of fishing lines on endangered species.

- So fishing lines should be redesigned so that albatrosses and other seabirds are not attracted to them.

- So there needs to be a better policing of the use of longlining.

And so on. There are no obvious limits to the number of inferences that could be drawn. (You might care to think of a further ten, or 20, or more.) All of the above would fit with the reasons-side of the argument in that each of them could be inferred from the claims made. But none is logically required. The connections on our Lego brick conclusion are still not entirely all covered. The significance of this point can be illustrated by looking at the next argument.

> All adult albatrosses have a large wing span.
> This bird is an adult albatross.
> So it must have a large wing span.

As you can see, the conclusion is a logical consequence of the two reasons acting together. It is not that the conclusion is probably true: it *must be true if the reasons are*. This is an important proviso. We could make claims that weren't true and end up with a conclusion that also wasn't.

> All cats have black fur.
> Billy is a cat.
> So Billy has black fur.

Though the second claim might be true, the first isn't, so the conclusion isn't.

Where the reasons are true, then our reasons-side Lego brick has two connections that fit exactly with the conclusion, as with the argument we saw above.

> Since all adult albatrosses have a large wingspan and this bird is an adult albatross, it must have a large wingspan.

This feeling of a perfect fit between the two sides is taken away when the inference-side is inadequate, given the content of the reasons-side.

> All adult albatrosses have a large wingspan.
> This bird is an adult albatross.
> So it might have a large wingspan.

This conclusion is simply too weak.

$$R \to C$$

The reasons need (require) a bigger conclusion. This is a strange feeling. For much of the time in Critical Thinking, we're looking at the relationship between the two sides of an argument as one where the reasons-side could always do with a bit of strengthening (as with the albatrosses example).

What about the next version?

> All adult albatrosses have a large wingspan.
> This bird has a large wingspan.
> So it must be an albatross.

Does this work, such that the conclusion is required?

As you can see, it doesn't. In the first example, the second claim was that this bird fell into the category of adult albatrosses. Because of this we had to conclude that it had the stated feature of such birds, viz., that it had a large wingspan. In the version just above, the second claim puts the bird into the category of those with a large wingspan (a category that includes all adult albatrosses). But this category will also include eagles, condors and so on, so we can't conclude that the bird has to be an albatross.

DEDUCTIVE ARGUMENTS

What we can see is that a combination of truth and structure or form of an argument creates a very different type of inference. We're now into deductive rather than inductive arguments.

You will sometimes see the term **syllogism** used when looking at particular types of argument. To simplify what is meant by this term, the first thing to note is that a syllogism consists of two reasons which together lead to the conclusion. It is, however, more than this. Each reason in a syllogism has one term in common with the conclusion, and one term in common with the other reason. Looking again at an earlier example should clarify this.

> All *albatrosses* have *a large wingspan*.
> **This bird** is an *albatross*.
> So **this bird** must have *a large wingspan*.

Syllogisms come in various forms. We'll meet some of them below.

DILEMMAS: REAL AND FALSE

Faced with a dilemma, we are concerned with having to decide between two options. We'll look at this aspect of a dilemma when we look at decision making in Chapter 4, but the term is also used to describe certain argument types. Again we're focusing on the structure of an argument.

Look at the next argument.

> Either the Prime Minister is telling the truth that there are no links between his party and the property development company Skyscrape UK or he is deliberately misinforming the public. It cannot be that he would risk lying about this link (in case he was ever found out to have done so), so he must be telling the truth.

This argument starts with a dilemma, thus giving only two possibilities: either the Prime Minister is telling the truth or he is not. Then there is a premise or reason given in order to draw the conclusion. Before we say more about this type of reasoning, let's be sure we can see what the form of the argument is.

If we give the letters A and B for the components of the argument, we can see that it has the following form.

> Either (A) the Prime Minister is telling the truth that there are no links between his party and the property development company Skyscrape UK or (B) he is deliberately misinforming the public. (Not B) It cannot be that he would risk lying about this link (in case he was ever found out to have done so), so (A) he must be telling the truth.

Put very baldly, the structure is:

A or B
Not B
Therefore A

You can see that A is a necessary (logical) consequence of the two previous claims. The same thing is going on in the next argument.

> Either the Government will have to risk unpopularity by putting up taxes to pay for people to draw pensions by the age of 65, or we have to expect to work

beyond that age (to 68 or more). The Government can't afford to risk being unpopular as a result of putting up taxes for this purpose, so people will have to work beyond 65.

The structure amounts to the same, even though there is one difference.

A or B
Not A
Therefore B

The difference is unimportant. The order in which the alternatives are presented does not affect the nature of the argument. The conclusion must follow.

This form of argument is, then, an example of what is called a **deductive argument**. We can go further and say that arguments of this type are deductively valid in that, if their reasons are true, the conclusion has to also be true. You can see why. If it is true that we have (only) either option A or B, and if one option is not the case, the other one must be the case.

Technically, what we have in this instance is what's called a 'disjunctive syllogism'. This is because the 'either A or B' statement is called a disjunction.

But what if there is a problem, not with the form, but with the content? The most obvious way in which there could be a problem with the content is if there is more than A or B to choose from. In other words, the dilemma we saw in the above arguments isn't a dilemma with only these two choices. There could be C or D or…

In this case, the conclusion is problematic because the reasons are not correct. This is an example of what is called a 'false dilemma'. You are likely to have met this before in looking at what's called 'restricting the options'. This is a type of flawed argument, in which the author presents only x options even though there's more than x available. Faced with the above argument about pensions, for example, we could say that other options could be: 'We could reduce the level of pension paid at 65, but still allow people to retire at that age' or 'We could encourage more people to pay into private pension schemes so that they can retire at 65'.

But if we are satisfied that the reasons given do not amount to a false dilemma and that they are therefore correct, then the conclusion must follow and the argument must then be valid. You will find this word 'valid' used very loosely. Some teachers of Critical Thinking use it to mean 'a good argument', without understanding that the validity of an argument derives from its structure.

Another clear example is this argument.

> The police said yesterday that, within 24 hours, they would either charge the woman with murder and keep her in custody or release her without charge. She was seen being dropped off at her house by a police car this afternoon. So she has not been charged with murder.

The structure is as before.

> Either A or B
> Not A
> Therefore B

If the police correctly presented the two options that they had, then the conclusion must follow. The argument is deductively valid.

IMPLICATION

There are other forms of argument that are deductively valid. Implication is one of them. This has a structure with a hypothetical form.

> If we put up taxes to pay for people to draw their pension at the age of 65, then people won't have to work beyond that age. Taxes in fact are going to be increased to pay for people to be able to draw their pensions at 65, so people won't have to work beyond that age.

The structure of this argument can be given as follows.

> If A is true, then B is true.
> A is true.
> So B is true.

In such arguments, A is called the **antecedent** and B is called the **consequent**. There will always be two reasons and a conclusion.

> R(1): (A) If we put up taxes to pay for people to draw their pension at the age of 65, then (B) people won't have to work beyond that age.

R(2): (A) Taxes are going to be increased to pay for people to be able to draw their pensions at 65.

C: (B) So people won't have to work beyond that age.

The reasons have to include a statement that the truth of one thing is dependent on the truth of something else (as in R(1)). When the antecedent is shown to be true, then the consequent has to be also because of the structure of the argument.

Implication is therefore a form of argument which is deductively valid. Those of you who like to use technical terms might like to refer to this form of argument by its other name, which is *modus ponens*. This means 'mode (of argument) that affirms'. You can see why: we are affirming (stating as a fact) that A is true. You can see why this form of argument is also referred to as 'affirming the antecedent'.

We need to be careful, however, that we haven't mistaken a different form of argument for implication. The next type of argument structure has perhaps a deceptive appeal.

AFFIRMING THE CONSEQUENT

As we have seen, implication gives us an argument that is deductively valid. Any argument that has the form of implication will have a conclusion that is true if the reasons it is drawn from are also true. But a shift in the structure can produce a very different result.

If we put up taxes to pay for people to draw their pension at the age of 65, then people won't have to work beyond that age. People won't have to work beyond the age of 65, so taxes must be going up.

This has the following structure.

If A is true, then B is true.
B is true.
So A is true.

This form of argument is not deductively valid. The truth of A does not depend on the truth of B: it is the other way round. The relationship between A and B cannot simply be reversed as if the order of the argument doesn't matter. There could be other reasons why people won't have to work beyond the age of 65. Perhaps lots of people have joined private pension schemes, which will reduce the need for the State to pay people's pensions at the early age of 65.

The next two examples further highlight the crucial difference between implication and affirming the consequent.

> If fast food companies didn't offer toys with their children's meals, then children would be less likely to choose these meals. Fast food companies will no longer be allowed to offer toys with their children's meals, so children will be less likely to choose these meals.

> If fast food companies didn't offer toys with their children's meals, then children would be less likely to choose these meals. Children are now less likely to choose these meals, so the companies no longer offer toys with them.

You will have seen that the first example is a deductively valid argument. The truth of B depended on the truth of A. The truth of A was established, so that of B was also shown. The second example affirmed the consequent, so is not a valid form of argument. The truth of A did not depend on the truth of B, so the conclusion about the truth of A could not be drawn. (It could be, for example, that children are deciding to eat differently, having listened to various anti-junk food campaigns.)

CHAIN ARGUMENTS

We have so far looked at two forms of deductively valid arguments (and one invalid one). Now we're going to look at a third valid form.

Chain arguments are sometimes called **hypothetical syllogisms**. They are an extension to the type of hypothetical form that we saw in implication. In a chain argument, another link (so to speak) is added to the sequence of the argument. Here is an example.

> If global warming is taking place, then we can expect sea levels to rise. If sea levels rise, large parts of coastal areas in some countries will disappear. So, if global warming is taking place, we can expect widespread flooding of large parts of coastal areas in some countries.

You can see why this form of argument is called **chain argument**. The structure makes clear the links between the beginning and the end.

> If A, then B.
> If B, then C.
> So, if A, then C.

The truth of C comes from the truth of B, whose truth comes from A.

Problems can arise in chain arguments when the form of the argument *appears* to be that of a chain, but when at least one link is broken by a shift in the meaning of the terms that are used. It is clear that if we are using A, B and C to refer to statements, then the statements must be equivalent. Where they are not, we have the problem of equivocation (sometimes referred to as conflation). In this problem, the author takes two (or more) terms to mean the same thing, though they do not.

> When we look at fuel prices in various countries, we find that motorists in the UK pay more for their fuel than those in most other countries, especially those in the US (where prices are about a third of those in the UK). But, if fuel prices weren't so high in the UK, then more people would use their vehicles for inessential journeys. If that were to happen, then the UK would have much higher vehicle emissions than it already does. Thus, if the costs of motoring in the UK weren't about the highest in the world, then its air quality would suffer more than it already does from vehicle emissions.

Though this argument has the look of a chain argument, the author has wrongly taken one part of the argument as if it is equivalent to another. This is 'if fuel prices weren't so high' and 'if the costs of motoring in the UK weren't about the highest in the world'. Though the two are similar, they're not equivalent. The cost of fuel is only one part of the cost of motoring (other parts include the cost of the vehicles themselves, the cost of insurance, government tax, any toll charges and so on).

DENYING THE CONSEQUENT

We looked above at an invalid form of argument which is called 'affirming the consequent'. We now look at a valid form of argument called 'denying the consequent'. This is sometimes referred to by its Latin name of *modus tollens*. Just as *modus ponens* meant 'mode that affirms', this means 'mode that denies'. We shall see why. In some ways, arguments of this type can look problematic rather than valid.

> If international aid works in improving the economies of the poorest countries, then these economies will have been improved by now. However, the economies of the poorest countries haven't improved, so international aid doesn't work in this way.

The structure of this argument is as follows.

If A, then B
Not B
Therefore not A.

This has the look of the invalid form of argument 'affirming the consequent' (if A, then B, B is true, therefore A). But the crucial difference is that the consequent (B) is denied rather than affirmed.

As with all the other forms of valid argument that we have considered, the truth of the conclusion requires the truth of the reasons. Thus the relationship between the antecedent and the consequent needs to be such that the only way for the consequent to be true is for the antecedent to be true. If we could deny the consequent without there being any significance for the antecedent, then this argument form would not be valid.

> If the police are going to be able to reduce organised crime, then they need to infiltrate the various gangs that commit the crime. They haven't been able to infiltrate these gangs, so they're not going to be able to reduce organised crime.

This argument has the right structure for a valid argument. Yet it would be problematic if there are ways that the police are going to be able to reduce organised crime that don't involve infiltrating the gangs. For example, they could get some gang members to 'grass' on those higher up in exchange for shorter sentences (as is done in the US). In this example, then, the reason isn't true, so neither is the conclusion.

DENYING THE ANTECEDENT

We also need to watch out for arguments in which it is the antecedent that is denied rather than the consequent. The next argument is an example of this.

> If the police are going to be able to reduce organised crime, then they need to infiltrate the various gangs that commit the crime. The police aren't going to be able to reduce organised crime, so they haven't been able to infiltrate these various gangs.

If A, then B
Not-A (A is not true)
So not-B (B is not true)

You can see that denying the antecedent is not a valid form of argument (it is sometimes referred to as 'inverse error'). In the above example, the police could have infiltrated various gangs even though, because of other reasons, they can't reduce organised crime.

It might be helpful to briefly summarise what we've been looking at with deductive arguments. The following table provides this summary.

	antecedent	consequent
affirmed	valid	invalid
denied	invalid	valid

EVALUATING INDUCTIVE ARGUMENTS

We have seen that an evaluation of deductive arguments looks to their form and the question of the truth of their premises. So is an evaluation of inductive arguments substantially different? In essence, it isn't. In both cases, we're looking to match the content of the reasons-side with the inference-side of the argument.

By 'matching' we mean looking at how far the contents of each side correspond. At the very least, we would ask these questions.

● Is there consistency between the two sides?
● Is the content of the reasons-side adequate for the inference?

With deductively valid arguments, we can find the much greater prize of sufficiency rather than the weaker version of adequacy. The premises will, as we have seen, be sufficient for the inference (indeed will require the inference). But, with inductive arguments, we are always chasing adequacy. We can say that the content of the reason-side gives us good (sometimes *very* good) or, of course, poor (sometimes *very* poor) reasons to believe the conclusion.

As you can see, there is an important sense in which the process of evaluating inference with inductive arguments is as much psychological as logical. Assuming we know the rules (and play by them) and assuming we know whether claims are true or not, we should be able to agree on whether an inference is valid or not. But with inductive arguments, the rules get fuzzy and all sorts of disagreements will follow. It is much more of a question of judgement, even if there is agreement on the question of the truth of factual claims.

Candidates for a UK assessment in Critical Thinking are told to write a 'convincing' argument on a subject. The question shouts itself: what is a 'convincing' argument? The fact that there is no necessary agreement on the answer to this question makes this instruction a very troubling one. We need to say to those who ask for a 'convincing' argument: 'convincing for whom?' Could I write an argument that would convince you that all people should be vegetarian? Could you write an argument that would convince me that Nazism had positive qualities?

This process of evaluation can operate in two ways. We can look at a claim or at claims and see what inference could be supported. We are asking: 'Where could this or these claims lead?' But we could reverse the process. We could look at a claim as a potential inference and consider what further claim or claims would be necessary for this inference.

We considered above that the process of inference can be understood as a psychological one. This is where a troublesome aspect lies as people might disagree on how this process would work. This disagreement will centre on the significance of the claim(s) from which an inference is drawn. Here's an example.

> Princess Diana was very interested in the campaign to get the use of landmines banned. Her death must have been linked to this interest as the way to stop her revealing information about those involved in the landmine trade.

Essentially we are discussing the significance of her interest in getting the use of landmines stopped. We are faced with the author's judgement that this interest was sufficient to explain Diana's death. The fact that she was interested in the landmine campaign, however, can be used as only one explanation among many others for her death in a car crash in 1997. In Chapter 4 we consider the problem of how we can describe anything as relevant to an inference. Here we can note the point that there isn't necessarily a clear relevance between Diana's campaign against landmines and her death. We exercise judgement here to question this relevance.

INFERENCE TO THE BEST EXPLANATION

But there is an account of inference called inference to the best explanation.[2] This has been proposed as a description of those inductive inferences that are acceptable. There are plenty of examples that can be used to show this.

> Adam has just walked into the office, with very wet clothes. It is raining heavily outside.

This very simple example illustrates what is meant by inference to the best explanation. We could obviously think of far more explanations for why Adam is wet. He could have had a bucket of water thrown over him. He could have recently walked into a river (or the sea). He could have taken a bath with his clothes on. But, with certain caveats in place (such as we are not in a spaceship, we are not in the middle of the Sahara and so on), we can take rain as the explanation for Adam's wet clothes. Even though we can come up with lots of different explanations (each of which might very occasionally be correct), the inference we have drawn can be taken to be the best one.

Inference to the best explanation reminds us that we can have a good deal of confidence in some inferences. We resist the complete scepticism by which we would have to say that, because there are other explanations, we just can't inductively infer anything with any confidence. Even when we do not have confidence in 'the best explanation', we could still have confidence that there are some explanations that are better than others. Thus we don't have to avoid drawing any inductive inference at all. We just need to ensure that we've applied some evaluation to the possible alternative explanations in order to have, at the very least, better explanations.

It's all very well, of course, to look for the best (or better) explanations and to draw (and accept) inferences from them. But there will be many situations in which our knowledge appears sufficient but turns out not to be. A good example is the Easter Island statues. These huge statues (known as 'moai') are famous for their over-large heads with distinctive features. They are tall and heavy (the tallest being almost 10 metres high and the heaviest being 86 tonnes), and were made from volcanic material. Various theories have been put forward to explain their presence on Easter Island. These include Erich von Däniken's explanation that extraterrestrials built them (after landing on a tiny island in the middle of the Pacific), having also had a hand in the building of Stonehenge and various constructions in South America.

The most commonly accepted explanation up until 2010 was that the statues were being transported along roads in Easter Island but were abandoned by the roadside by the ancient Polynesians. This was first put forward by Thor Heyerdahl of Kon-Tiki fame. Recent research, however, shows this explanation to be centrally wrong. This research by archaeologists from the University of Manchester and University College London shows that the road system of the island was not constructed in order to transport statues, but that the statues were integral to the road system. The roads led from different parts of the island to the volcano, with the statues lining the roads and becoming more frequent nearer the volcanic cone. This is significant in that the people saw the cone as a sacred site.

This explanation gets considerable support from the discovery that all the statues were originally on platforms, showing that they were where they were intended to be. Two footnotes to this story are important. First, a British archaeologist, Katherine Routledge, had put forward this explanation as long ago as 1914 but it had been largely forgotten. Second, Thor Heyerdahl found evidence of the platforms but ignored it, believing so strongly in his transportation explanation.[3]

So what does this Easter Island example show us? It emphasises that inferences to the best explanation work very well when there are very strong grounds for believing that the best explanation has been identified. In cases where there might be confusing (indeed contradictory) evidence, then we would have to settle for an inference from a useful explanation. Heyerdahl's discovery of the statues' platforms pretty well contradicted his transportation explanation and so his inference should have been different. (He should have drawn an inference which fitted better with the evidence.)

We began this chapter with a little story to illustrate the importance of clarity of language in Critical Thinking. This importance will be picked up and developed in the next chapter.

NOTES

1. See my *Critical Thinking for Students*. How To Books, 2010. pp. 37–38.
2. P. Linton, *Inference to the Best Explanation*. Routledge, 2004.
3. 'Archaeologists upset theory about Easter Island statues', www.scientificblogging.com

CLARITY AND MEANING

In the previous chapter, we briefly considered the point that in looking at the possible significance of claims we need to consider the meaning of words used. This is not something that we do most of the time. Life would be slow and tedious if all the time people were saying 'it depends what you mean by'. But an important skill in Critical Thinking is knowing when to ask questions about the meaning of words used by an author.

DEFINING PROBLEMATIC TERMS

HAPPINESS AND LIFE-SATISFACTION

There are some obvious examples of problematic terms when we look at studies of happiness and life-satisfaction.

> Costa Rica has the highest average happiness in the world. So we should learn something from this happy nation.

There has been a lot of interest over the past few years in studying levels of happiness throughout the world. For example, there is a measure of happiness that gives us what's called the 'happiness index'. This index is used to produce the 'World Database of Happiness', which ranks 148 countries. (Some are excluded, such as North Korea and Turkmenistan. You could consider why.) Happiness is measured on a scale of 0–10, and in 2009 the country with the top score of 8.5 was Costa Rica (just ahead of Denmark on 8.3, which had been top in previous surveys). The countries with the lowest score (2.6) are Togo and Tanzania (just behind Zimbabwe at 2.8).

DEFINITION OF HAPPINESS

The obvious question that you would want to ask if you were to look for inferences and explanations is 'How is happiness defined?'

For the World Database, the term 'happiness' is defined as 'the degree to which an individual judges the overall quality of his/her own life-as-a-whole favourably'.[1] Very usefully, the author of this part of the report then unpacks each of the terms within the definition in order to clarify them. Thus, for example, 'life-as-a-whole' is clarified to show that, though it 'covers past, present and anticipated experiences', it 'does not mean that all things ever experienced are given equal weight in the evaluation'.

APPLYING THE DEFINITION TO PEOPLE

Another approach to this issue could be to look, not at countries, but at age groups. For example, in one study, it was found that 'life-satisfaction' peaked at the age of 74.[2] This might strike you as odd and it in fact attracted various media coverage. It may well be that the very term 'life-satisfaction' has a built-in tendency to get higher levels among the reasonably old (rather than the group termed the 'oldest old'). (This could be because of their ability to look back at various good things that have happened in their lives, but without the burden of declining capabilities and the prospect of being summoned by mortality.) However, it could be that very young children actually are the happiest/most life-satisfied, but that their 'life-satisfaction' cannot be measured in the same way. In this way, the definition of the term might, in part, explain the evidence.

HAPPY PEOPLE: HAPPY NATIONS?

Let's turn our attention back to the original argument.

> Costa Rica has the highest average happiness in the world. So we should learn something from this happy nation.

The author, as you can see, moves from stating that Costa Ricans have the highest average happiness score to describing Costa Rica as a 'happy nation'. Is this a legitimate move? Is a high average happiness *equivalent* to a happy nation? (An obvious problem could be that some deliriously happy people will shift the average upwards, even if there are not loads of them in a society. This distorting problem can be found in estimates of income distribution.)

WHAT IS A 'NATION'?

This brings us to another definitional issue. What is a 'nation'? In this argument, the term seems to be used to describe the population of the country. We have a high average happiness score for the individuals of a country, so the country or nation is a happy one. So is a 'nation' simply the sum of its population, however small or large?

Here is Lee Kuan Yew, the Minister Mentor of Singapore, talking about his country in 2010.

> Singapore is 'few hundred years' shy of being a nation. 'It's a nation in the making.'

So why isn't Singapore already a 'nation'? Have a look at the two definitions below from the Oxford English Dictionary.

> A nation is 'a large aggregate of people united by common descent, history, culture, or language, inhabiting a particular state or territory'.

> A country is 'a nation with its own government, occupying a particular territory'.

So is Singapore, on this basis, not even a country? (It is, of course.)

MEANING AND DOUBLE MEANING

This example illustrates the point that, in looking for possibly problematic terms, there might well be others beyond the obvious.

Why should we spend time worrying about the meaning of terms? One of the central features of Critical Thinking is the recognition of the importance of clear thinking. We can't get very far with looking at claims and inferences from them if we are confused as to their meaning (or if we confuse by using words whose meaning is problematic).

Here is a nice example of a word's double meaning. There was a cartoon in the *Economist* of 16 May 2009 in response to a report that suggested that coral reefs were in considerable danger as a result of various activities such as fishing, tourism and building. In the cartoon, a fish calls out to other marine creatures:

'Bad news! Recent reports say our coral reefs are in critical danger.'

This shocks other marine creatures who then respond:

Turtle: 'Oh dear.'
2nd Fish: 'Somebody needs to do something.'
3rd Fish: 'Maybe Man will save us...'
Octopus: 'Yes!! After all, Man is responsible.'
4th Fish: 'Funny...I wouldn't use "Man" and "Responsible" in the same sentence...'

As you can see, the cartoon captures well the two separate meanings of the word 'responsible' as 'reliable' and 'accountable'.

Many problematic terms are used frequently in newspapers, magazines and official reports. We'll look at some of these in order to see how a lack of clarity in meaning can lead to a lack of clarity in argumentation.

FREQUENTLY USED PROBLEMATIC TERMS

ETHNIC MINORITY

What sort of problems do we encounter in using this term?

- Are really big 'ethnic minorities' still minorities (that need protection)?
- How small does an 'ethnic minority' have to be before it can be ignored? (As a percentage of the whole population? As a numerically very small group?)
- How permanent does an 'ethnic minority' have to be to be given a legal status?

Before we go any further, you're obviously wanting to make the following point.

Regardless of the size or permanence of an 'ethnic minority', how do we define the term?

Indeed, you're right. And the more we seek to nail the term down, the more problematic it becomes.

- Is it defined by DNA? If so, what about intermarriage? What about adoption? How far back do we want to go in looking at ancestry?

- Is it defined by language? So are all native speakers of other languages ethnic minorities? What about a country in which routinely more than one language is used (Singapore or India, for example)?

- Is it defined by status? If so, what status? Is Roman Abramovich (the owner of Chelsea football club) a member of the Russian ethnic minority in the UK? If so, what significance does this have?

- Is it defined simply in terms of a group with a recognisably distinct culture (including religion) which is a minority? But what happens when no one group is in a majority (a situation predicted for two UK cities – Leicester, by 2019, and Birmingham by 2024)?

- Is it defined by how recently the group arrived? The problem is that 'Go back far enough, and everyone moved somewhere from somewhere else.'[3]

As you can see, the use of the term 'ethnic minority' in claims and arguments is inevitably going to be problematic. For example, consider the following claim.

> There should be greater awareness of the needs of ethnic minorities in the education system.

You'll no doubt want to seize upon this claim like a ravenous dog, tearing it word from word. Apart from the vagueness of the term 'ethnic minorities', there's also the very troubling 'awareness' and 'needs' and even 'the education system'. The claim becomes, then, one without a useful meaning.

THE EFFECTS OF CLIMATE CHANGE

As you puzzle over these meanings, here's another problematic term. We're all used to hearing about climate change. But, even if we could agree on what the term means, can we agree on specific examples of its effects? For example, in 2009, the Global Humanitarian Forum published 'Human Impact Report: Climate Change – Anatomy of a Silent Crisis'. This report estimated that 325 million people are seriously affected by climate change every year and that, by 2030, this number could increase to 660 million.

But what counts as an example of the effects of climate change? In May 2009, Cyclone Aila hit Bangladesh and India's state of West Bengal. Hundreds were killed and at least half a million were made homeless as a result. So was this cyclone the result of global warming or was it just one of the cyclones that could be expected to hit that part of Asia? Without being able to answer this question, we can't usefully assess the numbers given in this report in terms of climate change.

FUTURE GENERATIONS

We've just considered a problem with predicting the effects of possible climate change. We're now going to look at a term that very much fits with the many problems of prediction. This is 'future generations'.

You might say that this is a pretty straightforward term because it simply refers to generations beyond the present ones. But, as we'll see, the term is far from being a straightforward one. Here's the first question.

> Do 'future generations' include those just being born, born in the past five years or born in the past ten years?

If we say 'no' to this question, do we keep having to change who the future generations are? If they're not those alive now (even if they're a few hours/days/weeks/months/years old), then are they those about to be born in the next few hours/days/weeks/months/years? You will see that things are slipping through our fingers. A two year old alive today will be part of the same generation as a child born two years from now. But where do we draw the line? A generation is usually counted as occupying 25 years, in the sense that the next one (their children) will start being created some time after then. So do we talk about future generations as those beyond that of present young people (up to the age of about 25)?

However, there are those who use the term 'future generations' to mean the present generation of young people. The President of the European Commission, José Barrosso, has written about the need to inspire 'future generations' and by this he is referring to the need to prepare the present group of young people for changes in employment and technology over the next 50 years.[4]

Perhaps we can clarify what we've been looking at by asking a second question.

> Are 'future generations' those who will be economically active in the future during a time when the present generations will not be?

You will recall from an example we considered earlier that those aged 74 appear to have a good chance of high life-satisfaction. But who is paying the bills? Those people working in various public sector jobs in the UK at the moment (such as teachers and civil servants) will expect their children (and grandchildren) to pay for their very generous pensions when they retire. Is this how we can use the term: the present young generation and their as yet unborn children? In this way, the term 'future generations' means both existing young people and their children and grandchildren.

But, given the usage of the term, we're making things a bit too easy. The term is used in many contexts and documents in a much more open-ended way. Here's an example.

> Wild flora and fauna constitute a natural heritage of great value that needs to be preserved and handed on to future generations.[5]

This suggests an on-going commitment from generation to generation, without any limit. The definition of the term would presumably not be seen as a problem because it includes all unborn generations.

Another example that is based on an open-ended position is a report published in 1997 by UNESCO (United Nations Educational, Scientific and Cultural Organisation): 'Declaration on the Responsibilities of the Present Generations Towards Future Generations'. It is a document worth reading from a Critical Thinking perspective in that it makes a whole series of claims that merit our attention. We'll have a look at some of them.

The document includes a list of 12 'articles' on the responsibilities to future generations. As a preamble to these articles, it gives various background claims. Here are some of them.

> Stressing that full respect for human rights and ideals of democracy constitute an essential basis for the protection of the needs and interests of future generations...

> Determined...to create such conditions as will ensure that the needs and interests of future generations are not jeopardized by the burden of the past, and to hand on a better world to future generations...

> Resolved to strive to ensure that the present generations are fully aware of their responsibilities towards future generations...

These background claims provide a rich source for evaluation. For example, the first one is claimed rather than argued for, even though it is so huge (especially with the words 'essential basis', thus making the 'full respect for human rights and the ideals of democracy' a necessary part of the 'protection of the needs and interests of future generations'). It's also interesting to see that present generations have a responsibility to pass on a 'better world to future generations'. This raises many questions about how and in what ways 'better'. (Does it mean that existing generations have to make sacrifices for future generations? If so, what sacrifices and to what extent? And, of course, which of the present generations has to make the sacrifices?)

You will have seen that UNESCO uses the plural 'present generations'. This raises a number of questions taking us back to where we started as to who is counted in 'present' and 'future' generations.

Beyond these points of evaluation about the claims that are made, you will see that, for UNESCO, the difficult problem of defining future generations is avoided: future generations are simply future generations. (Though the problem is avoided, the problem, of course, remains.)

So what responsibilities do the present (non-future) generations have to those of the future? The twelve articles include the following.

Article 1

The present generations have the responsibility of ensuring that the needs and interests of present and future generations are fully safeguarded.

This raises many interesting questions about the responsibilities of 'present generations' to themselves. Is this concerned with the responsibility of those present generations who are able to influence policies and practices to those who can't (most notably, the very young)?

Article 5

2. The present generations should ensure that future generations are not exposed to pollution which may endanger their health or their existence itself.

3. The present generations should preserve for future generations natural resources necessary for sustaining human life and for its development.

4. The present generations should take into account possible consequences for future generations of major projects before these are carried out.

Article 9
1. The present generations should ensure that both they and future generations learn to live together in peace...

You will have spotted the definitional problem here. If the 'present' and the 'future' generations should 'learn to live *together* in peace' (my emphasis), then who are the future generations?

2. The present generations should spare future generations the scourge of war.

This, of course, all sounds very worthy. But we have to keep coming back to definitional problems. If the present generations (however defined) have to preserve resources and take into account possible consequences of major projects, then we need to know which future generations we are talking about. This is because of a problem that won't go away. It's a problem that fits with another claim made in the preamble.

Bearing in mind that the fate of future generations depends to a great extent on decisions and actions taken today...

Quite simply, the fate of future generations is centrally in our hands in that we can choose whether or not to create the individuals that will be part of them. An example will show this. We hear a lot about the problems of over-population, such that there are calls to reduce the rate of population growth. The United Nations estimates that the world's population will be more than nine billion by 2050, and it has been argued that this is an unsustainable number. As Professor John Guillebaud has argued, 'We urgently need to stabilise and reduce human numbers. There is no way that a population of nine billion can meet its energy needs without unacceptable damage to the planet and a great deal of human misery.'[6] Thus Professor Guillebaud is arguing that future generations need to be restricted in size. If this is accepted, then we have the problem that our duty to future generations is not to create so many members of them.

This is a problem raised by the work of Derek Parfit.[7] He has argued that, if we have a moral obligation not to act in any situation where our action would make others worse off, then we have the devastating problem that acting to, for example, preserve the environment will deprive a future potential individual of life. This is because as soon as we make any present change, then the future changes (as with the 'butterfly effect', as described by Edward Lorenz). If we reduce the level of atmospheric pollution, then the chemistry of the environment changes, with the consequent butterfly effect of changes in the reproductive chemistry of people. Following these chemical changes, we will find that sperm x will reach egg x before sperm y (a race with a possible different result without the changes). Thus potential individual P1 never makes it beyond potential whereas potential individual P2 emerges, as a result of favourable chemistry, into actuality. So, by making the world better, we make it immeasurably worse for P1. And, if Professor Guillebaud has his way, many of the extra 200,000 extra human babies currently born each day will never be born.

Parfit's problem of the status of future generations is a central one for definitional work on this term. As we have seen, we are faced with the prospect of a series of possible future generations, each one of which will then have the potential to create a further series, and so on. The fact that you're reading this is significant in this context: the chances of you existing (being conceived) were very small, being based on a huge number of variables. Your biological parents were only two of these variables. So when the UK's Royal Society for the Protection of Birds (RSPB) produced an advertising campaign in 2009 consisting of a letter addressed to 'children of the future', we would have to respond by asking 'who are they?' Is it these children or those children or neither?

So, if the UNESCO document doesn't have the impact that the organisation hoped, would our potential Ps prefer not to be born in a world with over-exploited resources or to be born into such a world and take their chances in it?[8]

You might think that enough's enough: the future generations are simply those who will be born rather than those who might have been. On this basis, we might have various responsibilities to these as yet future children, grandchildren and so on, as they will have to theirs. Although the little voice from P1 asking for existence might still be heard...

FURTHER PROBLEMS OF DEFINITION

As Critical Thinkers, we should always be attuned to how definitional issues can affect claims and inferences from them. If we are going to evaluate arguments which go from *a* to *b* (or if we are going to produce such arguments ourselves), then we need to ask questions, when necessary, to clarify the content of *a* and *b*.

For example, if we think that the sale of fair-trade products should be encouraged, we would have to stop and ask what we mean by 'fair trade' (and, of course, what we mean by '*free* trade', to which proponents of fair trade are normally opposed). Or even what do we mean by 'trade'?

Here's another one. A six-year-old child in the US, Zachary Christie, was suspended from school in 2009 for bringing a knife into school.[9] This might seem a straightforward point in that, following incidents like the Columbine and Virginia Tech shootings, many schools in the US adopted a zero-tolerance policy on the possession of weapons on school grounds. The problem, however, was that Zachary, having just joined the Cub Scouts, was thrilled with his combined knife, fork and spoon as used by Cub Scouts. His suspension 'just seems unfair,' explained Zachary. So should a policy against the carrying of knives include implements like this? When is a knife not a knife? (Is the whole thing to do with purpose?)

If you can solve that one, think of the astronomers as they debated long and hard as to what is a 'planet'. You might remember that Pluto was downgraded from 'planet' to 'dwarf planet' in 2006. But you're probably already thinking that this still makes Pluto a 'planet'. This is indeed a problem. Just as a dwarf galaxy is still a galaxy and a dwarf star still a star, so a dwarf planet is presumably still (by definition) a planet.[10]

Here's another problem. In these days of ships being intercepted by pirates, especially those from Somalia, the question needs to be asked, 'What is a pirate? 'I believe the title of pirates should be given to those who come to our waters illegally,' said one Somalian 'pirate' from prison. He was referring to the foreign trawlers that over-fished the sea and to foreign ships that dumped toxic waste in the coastal waters.[11] Are both the captured 'pirate' and those who have damaged the resources of the Somalian coastal village communities all pirates? Is it a legal definition? A moral one? An economic one (as in 'video piracy')? Or what?

And then there's the hugely important problem of the meaning of 'death'. At what point can it be said that someone is 'dead'? This is one still being debated by doctors, representatives of religious groups and philosophers.[12] Over to them . . .

NOTES

1. See http://worlddatabaseofhappiness.eur.nl at section 2/1.
2. B. Baird et al., 'Life satisfaction across the lifespan: findings from two nationally representative panel studies', *Social Indicators Research*, February 2010.
3. 'Welcome home', www.economist.com, 22 October 2009.

4. 'Inspiring Future Generations', www.egovmonitor.com, 6 October 2008.
5. The Bern Convention, 'Council Decision 82/72/EEC, 3 December 1982'.
6. 'Overpopulation "is main threat to planet"', *Independent*, 7 January 2006.
7. D. Parfit, *Reasons and Persons (Part Four)*. Oxford University Press, 1984.
8. There is a useful discussion of this issue in A. D'Amato, 'Do we owe a duty to future generations to preserve the global environment?', *American Journal of International Law*, 190, 1990, p. 3. An imaginary lawyer representing possible future generations responds, 'My clients would rather live in whatever environment is left to them than not be born at all.'
9. 'It's a fork, It's a spoon, It's a…weapon?', *New York Times*, 12 October 2009.
10. See, for example, S. Eales, 'The fallen planet', *Prospect*, May 2007. For a critical discussion of the decision to demote Pluto (with an examination of the inconsistencies involved), see A. Ahuja, 'So, farewell planet Earth – is this the end of the world as we know it?', *The Times*, 13 November 2006.
11. 'Hostages a valuable commodity', *The Times*, 28 October 2009.
12. 'O death, when is they sting?', *Economist*, 2 October 2008.

DECISION MAKING – CHOICES
AND CRITERIA

EMPLOYING EVIDENCE TO CONSIDER 'WHAT IS THE GOOD SOCIETY?'

BRUCE ACKERMAN ON SOCIAL JUSTICE

In Bruce Ackerman's excellent book *Social Justice in the Liberal State*[1] various characters are on their way to another planet in order to set up a new community. They are required to spend the journey working out a moral framework for this new community, a framework which would result in a socially just community. There are certain ground rules for the debate between the members (who include 'Struggler', 'Manic', 'Depressive', 'Noble', 'Nazi' and some 'Junior' versions of these). The debate is chaired and refereed by the Commander. She reminds the members of the community of these ground rules whenever necessary.

These rules are rationality, consistency and neutrality. Rationality requires that a 'power-holder' gives a reason to justify an entitlement to a resource. Consistency requires that the reason given is consistent with any other reasons used. Neutrality requires that the power-holder cannot give reasons that assume that their conception of the 'good' is superior to others' conceptions and that, regardless of their conception of the 'good', that they are intrinsically superior to others.

You will have seen that these rules fit very well within Critical Thinking. We expect that positions are justified by reasons, reasons that are consistent with each other, and that an arguer can't simply fall back on saying, 'Well, I'm simply better than you are' (however tempting that might be).

EVIDENCE AND THE GOOD SOCIETY

Though philosophers and political theorists might argue about the nature of the good society, they will normally do so without focusing on evidence. But, of course, decision making about the good society, like any other decision making, is likely to be improved if evidence is considered. We could put this somewhat differently: decision making about the good society is a somewhat limited exercise if relevant evidence is not considered. As a result, it is instructive to approach such a decision-making exercise with a focus on evidence as a central part of it. For example, if we can find a country which is measurably happier than others (as we saw with Costa Rica), then we should have a look at evidence about that country. Thus instead of talking about a happy community or society in the abstract, we should look at relevant evidence about *real* happiness in *real* places.

The long-standing point that what are called 'ought' positions can't be drawn from 'is' positions is often used to play down the significance of evidence in moral decision making. For example, the decision whether or not to have capital punishment is often looked at in terms of possible deterrent effects, economic factors and procedural issues, but there are many who would stress that, way beyond all these points, is the central moral argument about whether it is right to kill someone (such that, regardless of the evidence, it either can be justified or it can't).

At the very least, though, 'oughts' are likely to be better decisions if they are based on evidence. A political theory which doesn't take into account political behaviour or the effects of certain policies in specific situations is an odd thing to be advocating.

SATISFACTION WITH LIFE

In the previous chapter we looked at how 'happiness' might be defined. We'll revisit this area to see how an evidence-based approach can help to make progress in decision making. Table 3.1 shows what have been termed 'Happy Life Years'. It presents not just the countries' 'satisfaction with life' scores that we considered earlier but also the life expectancy in these countries. These two measures are used to produce Happy Life Years, which thereby provide an estimate of 'how long and happy the average citizen will live in that nation'.

Table 3.1[2]

Country	Life satisfaction score (0–10)	Life expectancy (in years)	Happy life years
Costa Rica	8.5	78.5	66.7
Iceland	8.2	81.5	60.9
Denmark	8.3	77.9	65.0
Switzerland	8.0	81.3	65.0
Canada	8.0	80.3	64.0
Mozambique	3.8	42.8	16.4
Togo	2.6	57.8	15.1
Tanzania	2.6	51.0	14.4
Burundi	2.9	48.5	14.3
Zimbabwe	2.8	40.9	12.5

Though we don't want at this stage to get caught up with moral issues of what we should and shouldn't do, it seems reasonable to accept as a starting point that the more satisfied with life we are, the better it is. There's probably little point in using evidence to look for ways of making us less rather than more satisfied with our lives.[3] So we're interested in these figures, but what do they tell us?

You'll remember the point that we stressed earlier that evidence-claims are neutral until someone does something with them by drawing an inference from them. So the evidence on these countries sits there, so to speak, with no significance as yet.

The figures are interesting but is there a pattern that we can find, just by looking at them? There is one that you will have seen.

Countries that have a relatively low life expectancy also seem to have low satisfactions with life scores.

Although it's not as simple as that. In the table, Mozambique has a much lower life expectancy than Togo, but noticeably happier people. Similarly, Costa Rica has the happiest people but a lower life expectancy than other countries with high satisfaction scores. So perhaps the inference that comes from the pattern is that:

'It is better to have really satisfied years than slightly more but less satisfied years.'

Another pattern is that the high-performing countries in the Happy Life Years are countries north of the equator and the low-performing countries are all south of the equator. (Is there an inference that can be drawn from this?)

HAPPY YEARS, MONEY AND DEMOCRACY

What happens when we start to add in other evidence? Consider Table 3.2.

Table 3.2

Country	Life satisfaction	Life expectancy in years	Happy life years	Population (in millions)	GDP per head (US$)*	Democracy index rank**
Costa Rica	8.5	78.5	66.7	4.5	10,900	25 =
Iceland	8.2	81.5	60.9	0.3	39,600	2
Denmark	8.3	77.9	65.0	5.5	36,000	5
Switzerland	8.0	81.3	65.0	7.3	41,700	10
Canada	8.0	80.3	64.0	32.9	38,400	9
Mozambique	3.8	42.8	16.4	20.5	900	96
Togo	2.6	57.8	15.1	6.5	900	164
Tanzania	2.6	51.0	14.4	39.7	1,400	99
Burundi	2.9	48.5	14.3	8.1	300	107
Zimbabwe	2.8	40.9	12.5	13.2	332	147 =

*   GDP per head is given in US$. Gross Domestic Product is a measure of all of the output produced by economic activity in a country.[4]
** The Democracy Index ranks 167 countries in the world against various measures of democracy, such as the degree of civil liberties and the quality of the electoral system.[5]

If we were looking to make pronouncements on what the good society might look like, we now have more information. Ackerman's space-travellers would very much benefit from puzzling over evidence such as this, rather than just fretting about conceptions of justice.

So what might this evidence be telling us?

- Though the happiest country is not the most democratic, there is certainly a notice-able correlation between a high rank on the democracy index and a high life satisfaction score. A strongly supported inference could therefore be that 'highly democratic countries have high levels of life satisfaction'. The country that scores the highest on the democracy index is Sweden with a score of 9.88 out of a maximum 10.00; it is ranked 7th on the happy years score. North Korea is the bottom performer on the democracy index with a score of 1.03 and is not featured in the life satisfaction study.

- The level of GDP per head tends to be positively correlated with happiness scores. Though Costa Rica rather spoils the picture with a relatively modest figure, the other high happiness-scoring countries have very high GDP scores. The correlation between democracy and economic wealth is also to be noted.

- The size of the population of a country also appears to be significant. The top four countries for happy years have populations below 7.5 million. This might well be telling us something significant, although there is clearly not a straightforward causal relationship here, as the example of Togo shows.

It is likely that you will be able to find other possible correlations from these figures. But if we were being pushed to draw an inference from the evidence we have here, it would be something like the following.

Happy societies are very likely to be economically well developed and highly democratic.

Countries with low levels of happiness tend to be economically undeveloped and undemocratic.

As a result, if we value happiness, we value democracy. Ackerman's seekers after the just society might well stop and look at these inferences carefully. (Although they'd find themselves agreeing with them via other ways of thinking about the issue.)

Of course, things can get messy (as in any inductive reasoning). Qatar has the second-highest GDP per head in the world, 50.6 happy years, and yet scores a very lowly 142 on the democracy index. However, Luxembourg takes us back to safer inference with the highest GDP per head in the world, 60.7 happy years, and an impressive 7th on the democracy index.

THE ROLE OF CRITICAL THINKING IN DECISION MAKING

All of this evidence examination shifts the focus for Critical Thinking. Instead of carping from the sidelines – 'that doesn't follow' and suchlike – the subject is placed at the centre, with other relevant disciplines knocking on the door and asking, 'We'd like some help with this please.' Of course this assumes that the person who answers the door marked 'Critical Thinking' is competent. A health warning about the instant experts who set up shop and sell dubious products should be clearly shown on this door: 'Watch out for quacks'.

Fortunately, for the anxious enquirer who knocks on the door, there is some reassurance. Critical Thinking not only brings skills in evaluating the significance of evidence. It also brings skills of clarification and criteria selection. These can be listed. Critical Thinking can:

- contribute to the clarification of the nature of the decision to be made;
- clarify the range of choices available;
- help to produce the criteria that can/should be used in evaluating the choices available;
- help to select evidence on the basis of relevance;
- look at the possible significance of any evidence that is seen as relevant;
- improve any attempt to apply ethical positions to decision making (having prepared the ground by clarification, criteria selection and evidence evaluation).

Before we start exploring these points, it's useful to consider that very often what we refer to as a decision can also be seen as a recommendation. When somebody says that something should happen/be done, then they're recommending this course of action. But it can also be seen as a decision that's been made: this course of action is best. However, there is a distinction between the two. Someone might recommend that a particular course of action be taken. It becomes a decision once that recommendation is accepted or rejected (or modified).

CLARIFICATION OF THE DECISION'S NATURE

The first area that we'll look at is the clarification of the nature of the decision to be made. You will remember the Chinese saying quoted in Chapter 1: 'Simplicity is a blessing'. It might look as if we're going to fly in the face of this with what we're about to do, in that we're going to take a simple decision-claim and then reveal its complexity. But the point will be shown that the simplicity of a claim is often no more than a surface simplicity.

CLARIFICATION – AN EXAMPLE: LEARNING FOREIGN LANGUAGES

Here is a simple decision-claim.

All children should learn a foreign language.

It looks simple enough. It's a familiar enough decision-claim (or recommendation), and it would seem uncontroversial. But what exactly might it mean? We're again into the meaning of words. Let's look at each of them.

All

What does this mean? It suggests that, without exception, children should learn a foreign language. But does this mean 'all', without taking into account any disabilities that might or will stop the acquisition of a foreign language? (It is clear that some children have very limited language-acquisition skills.) So this decision-claim should be reworded to one of two.

Virtually all children should learn a foreign language.
Most children should learn a foreign language.

The second of these is the weaker and might be too weak. The first is probably better in that it requires that only a very small proportion of children are not included.

Children

Oddly, it is far from obvious what this means. The Oxford Dictionary includes 'infant', 'offspring' and 'pupil' in its definition. Does this mean then that children should include those of pre-school age? If so, how young? Should parents and other carers be using some foreign language words in their everyday vocabulary? If so, how many and how often? And what sort of words?

There is evidence that children who are brought up with more than one language being spoken to them not only have improved linguistic abilities but also better analytical and problem-solving skills. This occurs where either both parents/carers speak more than one language or where one of the parents/carers speaks one language and the other another language. But presumably nobody is going to make a decision *requiring* that infants have more than one language spoken to them. It couldn't even be required that all pre-school children have access to some foreign language acquisition programme as not all pre-school children have pre-school education.

So let's take the word 'child' to mean those of school age, whatever that happens to be. This avoids all of the problems given above.

Our decision has so far been changed to:

Virtually all children of school age should learn a foreign language.

Even this, of course, has a further question that needs to be answered: 'When should this continue until?' Should children throughout their school life learn a foreign language? Any answer to this question will need to consider the next word, which is:

Learn

This is a very difficult one as it could have a variety of meanings. It clearly involves the acquisition of some words from a foreign language and the ability to know how to use them. But what is the purpose of this acquisition? Should children learn such that they can speak the foreign language with some fluency? What degree of fluency? Should they be able to read this language with some fluency? What degree of fluency? What should they able to read – newspapers, magazines, reports, books? Should they be able to listen to native speakers and understand them? (To what degree?)

This central question of the purpose of learning a foreign language can also be seen in terms of the more general question: Why should children learn a foreign language? Is it for when they travel abroad as tourists? Is it so that they can work abroad? Is it in case they want to do business abroad? Is it so that they can read foreign language material (newspapers, magazines, books, etc.). Is it all of these?

Of course, this discussion envisages a situation in which a child is learning a language that is not already spoken to any great extent in their society. If one looks at a country like Singapore, we have children faced with the need to have some degree of competence in at least two languages – English and their mother tongue. For effective participation in a country like Singapore, people need a high level of competence in both English and Mandarin. However, neither of these might be their mother tongue.

This then brings us to the final term.

Foreign language

The obvious question is, 'Which one?' For many people in countries around the world, English is the obvious choice, given its status as the main international language. But for English-speakers which other language should it be? French? This is obviously useful as one of the languages of the European Union. Spanish? This is useful given its widespread use in South America. Mandarin? Given the size and growing importance of China, this makes some sense. Arabic? The large number of countries that have this language makes the case for this a useful one.

Of course, this approach could well be seen as over-restrictive. Perhaps, as in many European countries (but not the UK), at least two foreign languages should be taught.

Anyway, what counts as 'foreign'? In countries that use more than one language (for example, India, Switzerland, Singapore), this has a particular significance. It highlights that perhaps we should reword the question.

Virtually all children of school age should learn at least one language.

This last point takes us back to a previous discussion on the purpose of learning a language. Unless this purpose is made clear, the answer to the question of which language cannot be given. Is it just that learning an additional language is good for the brain, by developing connections and pathways? (The learning of Latin is a good example. Few people now speak this language on a daily basis, but it has been shown to have benefits for developing children's thinking.) Is it that children should learn the language(s) that would be the most useful (for their careers, for example)? But how we would know this? A child might be very successful in learning Spanish only to find that their work takes them to China.

As we can see, Critical Thinking is something like a dog with a bone. By asking lots of questions, it just keeps gnawing away at a proposed decision-claim in order to help to clarify the nature of the decision. So, if a government decides that

All children should learn a foreign language

then it would need to answer these kinds of questions before it went further into questions like funding, timetabling, recruitment of teachers, and so on.

This method is very useful in pulling the decision-maker(s) back from specifying the content of the decision without reflecting on what they want to achieve. It could be that, in this case, what they wanted to achieve was for (virtually) all school children to have some ability in a foreign language. Our questions moved them away from this overly vague (so not a good) position.

As we saw in Chapter 2, trying to reduce ambiguity is one of the many important features of Critical Thinking. This emphasis on clarity is very useful before we take the process any further.

CLARIFICATION – AN EXAMPLE: FOREIGN AID

Let's look at another decision-claim.

Spending on foreign aid should be protected.

This is a familiar position. It seems that it's meant to go without saying that foreign aid shouldn't be reduced. But there's a word literally in the middle of this sentence which is highly problematic and therefore requires clarification. What is meant by 'aid'?

It might seem obvious in an uncritical Bob Geldoff/Bono way that aid means giving at the very least, giving cash normally, but giving without strings. So does it also mean any of the following?

- Providing low interest loans.
- Providing loans with no interest payable.
- Investing in the economy of a country.
- Building roads, hospitals, schools, etc.
- Bribing local officials in order to be able to supply goods.
- Bribing government officials to be allowed to bring humanitarian supplies into the country.
- Being given rights to valuable minerals in exchange for goods supplied by 'donor' country.
- Building and/or improving infrastructure such as railways with labour and equipment supplied by 'donor' country.
- Building large projects such as presidential palaces and sports stadiums.

All of these might be counted as examples of 'aid' in the sense that something happens in the aided country which might count as an improvement. But what if the aid benefits the aiding country more than the one that's aided? Is this still 'aid'? (Or is it exploitation, or even 'trade'?) What if improving a railway system is a form of investment which ties in the aided country to buying equipment (engines, rolling stock, etc.) from the supplying country? What if 'aid' benefits only the political/economic/military élite?

In other words, does 'aid' have any limits to what it means? (Or does it mean what the person/organisation/country giving aid says it means?)

We're going to be looking in detail at how evidence can help in decision making later, but there's already a way in which it can inform at this stage. There is evidence that in some countries aid simply has had the effect of the aided government reducing its own expenditure. Thus there have been cases in which aid for a country's health care services resulted in the country reducing its own health care spending by an equal amount. With regard to health care, the result is, of course, that spending on it stays the same. So is this 'aid' in any meaningful way? (Perhaps it might be if the money saved was spent on other useful programmes.)

CLARIFICATION – AN EXAMPLE: VAGUENESS FROM POLITICIANS

This emphasis on clarification of terms used often sits uncomfortably with pronouncements by political leaders. For example, as I write, I'm hearing that the UK Government is going to put 'the family at the centre' of its policies. This might be quite nice if I had any idea of what it meant. Neither of the two big terms has been clarified. What is meant by 'the family'? Is it the nuclear or the extended family? If it is the extended family, how extended is it taken to be? So should children look after their elderly parents (rather than have them admitted to nursing homes)? And what might 'the centre' mean? That all policies will be 'family-friendly'? (Sorry for that one – it's a term that's often used and, without specification of meaning and thus content, it gets us nowhere.) So the promise of putting 'the family at the centre' ends up, in the absence of clarification and detail, as one without significance.

Similarly, a policy offering us 'the big society' is not obviously meaningful. These examples illustrate nicely that no decision-making exercise can make much (any?) progress without a stern clarification of terms used. Without this, we do not know what decision we're meant to be considering.

This first section of the chapter has concentrated on achieving clarification of the general direction that is needed. If someone is looking to arrive at a decision with regard to a specific question, then clarification will literally clear the way for the examination of different approaches to achieving this.

CLARIFICATION OF THE RANGE OF CHOICES AVAILABLE

We have seen that any consideration of the range of choices available for making a decision needs to be based on the clarification that has gone before it. Without such clarification, there will be problems in producing the choices that might be available.

Hopefully it should be pretty clear how this would operate with something like an aid programme. If we haven't clarified what is meant by aid, how can we consider a range of choices in providing aid? For example, if aid doesn't include building palaces and sports stadiums, then this can't be part of the choices that are available. Similarly, if aid doesn't include allowing the aided country to choose how to spend the aid, then this also can't be a choice.

EXAMPLE: EARLY RELEASE FROM PRISON

We'll look at another example. During the 2010 UK election campaign, the Conservative Party spent a great deal of money on a poster campaign. One of these posters carried a photograph of the then Prime Minister, Gordon Brown, with the message 'I released 80,000 prisoners early'. The accompanying 'Vote for me.' was obviously meant to be an inference that was problematic. But the Critical Thinker would look at this poster and ask, 'So how many prisoners should have been released early?' A Critically Thinking alien visiting the UK at the time could have been forgiven for thinking that the Prime Minister was being criticised for not releasing more. 'Is that all?' the alien might have asked, having checked the imprisonment rate beforehand.

The policy of releasing prisoners before the end of their sentences was adopted in the UK long before the then Prime Minister came to power (and was certainly in place when the Conservative Party was in government), so the implied criticism of the numbers shouldn't necessarily be taken to mean that no prisoners should be released early. (Lord Archer, a prominent Conservative, certainly benefited from being released early from his prison sentence, despite an earlier protestation that no prisoner should be.)

CLARIFICATION OF THE TERM 'EARLY RELEASE'

If we want to consider the range of choices for an early release programme, as usual we can see that we need to start with a clarification of the term.

What is meant by 'early' release?

This general question goes to the heart of the problem. It can be unpacked into specific questions.

● How 'early' is it? (A fixed percentage of the sentence? A percentage that varies according to the length of the sentence? A percentage that depends on the crime committed, the behaviour of the prisoner and so on?)

- Does/should it apply to all/most prisoners?
- Does early release involve a programme of continuing supervision for those who are released early?

This last question focuses us well on the significance of a word that might otherwise be ignored. What do we mean by 'release'? Does it refer only to a conditional status, involving significant restrictions on what the offender can do? For example, will the offender be tagged, required to report frequently to an official, subject to a curfew and so on?

We can see, from the above, that the poster with its message of about 80,000 'early releases' is telling us very, very little.

We can apply this initial clarification to an attempt to produce a range of choices for a policy on early release. The person knocking on the door asking for Critical Thinking help wants to be clearer about how to approach such a policy.

A CONTINUUM OF CHOICE

Some years ago, I introduced the idea of a continuum of choice when using Critical Thinking in decision making.[6] A continuum of choice is based on the idea that the variety of positions available for making a decision can be approached in terms of a continuum with the more extreme positions occupying either end. Using this with the idea of early release from prison we can see how the scope of such a programme changes as we move along the continuum.

A CONTINUUM OF CHOICE: EARLY RELEASE

Have no early release...have a range of early release programmes...have all prisoners (except those on whole-life sentences) eligible for early release.

We would need to unpack the middle choice in this continuum into specific decisions, but they would occupy the same place on the general continuum. However, when we start to provide detail, we can see that we get a continuum within a continuum. An example follows. (We read this with the understanding that at any choice, all those before it are also chosen. Thus, for example, the third choice would also include the first and second.)

> ...have an early release programme only for those prisoners with a perfect disciplinary record...have a limited early release programme for those prisoners with a very good disciplinary record...have a very limited early release programme for those prisoners with only an acceptable disciplinary record...have a very restricted early release programme for those prisoners with a poor disciplinary record...have a very highly restricted early release programme for those prisoners with unacceptable disciplinary record...

We would, of course, need to define the terms 'very good' and so on. We might also have to define what is meant by 'disciplinary record'. For example, does it include only those aspects of behaviour which were officially recorded or does it also include judgements made by prison staff?

Here's another continuum (in this case, part-continuum) within the continuum.

> ...have an early release programme for only those prisoners who haven't committed a violent crime...for only those prisoners with a low-level of violent crime...

And here's another one.

> ...for only those prisoners with a sentence of less than three years...less than four years...

And so on.

We could look at other factors, such as whether the prisoner has a job to go to, a settled accommodation to return to, expressed remorse, satisfactorily completed an offending-behaviour programme and so on. We could, of course, combine these different criteria into a series of positions.

> ...have an early release programme for only those prisoners with a perfect disciplinary record who didn't commit a violent crime...for those prisoners with a very good disciplinary record who didn't commit a violent crime...for those prisoners with an acceptable disciplinary record who didn't commit a violent crime...with a poor disciplinary record who didn't commit a violent crime...with an unacceptable disciplinary record who didn't commit a violent crime...

And yet more.

> ...have an early release programme for only those prisoners who didn't commit a violent crime and who have a perfect disciplinary record and a sentence of less than three years...for those prisoners who didn't commit a violent crime and who have a very good disciplinary record and a sentence of less than four years...

We'll be looking at how we might evaluate the positions on a continuum in the next section. However, before we do this, it will be worth stepping back and considering a bigger question. In doing this, we'll see that we can often gain a better insight into the nature of a decision by asking bigger questions.

LOOKING AT A BIGGER QUESTION: THE BEST SIZE OF THE PRISON POPULATION

In the case of the early release controversy, a bigger question is:

> What is the best size for the prison population?

This might seem to be a strange question. The following answer might be given.

> The best size is whatever is needed for the number of criminals who need putting in prison.

The Critical Thinker will gasp and splutter at this one. It raises more questions than it answers.

> How many offenders 'need putting in prison'? All of them? For how long should offenders be in prison?

You will see that we're back to definitions. What is meant by 'criminals'? All those who commit a crime? What do we mean by 'crime'? Do we include being caught speeding just over the speed limit? Do we include the theft of something of small monetary value? Do we mean evading tax? Dropping litter?

Some newspapers report favourably on any proposed building of more prisons. Some politicians use such building as a rallying cry – 'We'll build more prisons.' – and get enthusiastic applause. A politician announcing 'We'll close lots of prisons!' is likely to be greeted by a chorus of disapproval. So what's going on with the thinking that more prisons is a good thing?

We can see that the number of prison places needed is a complex issue, but it is clearly central to the issue of early release. The number of prison places needed is both affected by an early release policy and affects such a policy.

You will remember that we are very interested in the role of evidence in decision making, so let us look at the size of the prison populations in different countries. Table 3.3 shows the evidence on 11 countries. The lower the figure given in the World Ranking column, the higher the imprisonment rate.

Table 3.3[7]

World rank	Country	Prison population	Prisoners per 100,000 population
1	US	2,186,230	738
2	Russia	869,814	611
14	Singapore	15,038	350
18	South Africa	157,402	335
53	Costa Rica	7,782	181
83	UK	88,458	124
101	South Korea	45,882	97
121	Denmark	4,198	77
147	Iceland	119	40
151	India	332,112	30
155	Nepal	7,135	26

They are a very interesting set of figures. For one thing, we now have a wonderful correlation with the US having both the highest level of Nobel Prize winners and the highest imprisonment rate!

So what is the ideal imprisonment rate? Should the US be the model here, with 738 of its population for every 100,000 in prison? Or should it be Nepal, ranked the lowest, with only 26? Or should it be somewhere in between (why? where?)? Should it perhaps be outside of the range 26 to 738? Thus should it be fewer than 26 or more than 738?

As we can see, the notion that there is a figure that somehow represents the ideal imprisonment rate is a very slippery one. Would it help if we had some figures on violent crime? Let's look at murder to see if there's any useful pattern (see Table 3.4).

Table 3.4[8]

World rank	Country	Murder rate per 100,000 population
1	Colombia	62.7
3	South Africa	47.5
40	Costa Rica	5.7
44	US	5.6
51	India	3.7
52	Nepal	3.4
72	UK	2.1
100	Iceland	1.0
117	Singapore	0.5
122	Myanmar	0.2

The Myanmar (Burma) figure is interesting. It has a very, very low reported murder rate and the figures for imprisonment are 60,000 (one of very few countries with a nicely-rounded figure) with a rate per population of 120 and a world ranking of 86. These are virtually the same as the UK's prison figures. But we might doubt the accuracy of the evidence from Myanmar because of the considerable restrictions on access to information in that country. (So do the Myanmar figures tell us anything?)

Singapore presents an interesting case. Here is a country with a high imprisonment rate and a very low murder rate. Could we say that the latter is because of the former? (Or might it be because of its use of capital punishment?) So is an imprisonment rate of 350 per 100,000 the one to aim for? On that basis, the UK should imprison 210,000 people, significantly more than it does, if we take the murder rate to be very relevant in this context. The US, on the other hand, should imprison about half the number of people it currently does.

Iceland, however, gives an opposite picture to Singapore. It has one of the lowest imprisonment rates (40) and also one of the lowest murder rates (1), so we have an opposite correlation to that of Singapore. If we generalise from Iceland, then Singapore should imprison only 1,760 people, over 13,000 fewer than it does now. The UK should imprison only 24,000 people, almost 65,000 fewer than it does now.

You will have seen that Nepal sits just into the second half of the table for the murder rate even though it has the lowest imprisonment rate. Colombia with an astonishingly high murder rate needs, some might say, to increase its imprisonment rate from 134. Perhaps, on these figures, both countries should build more prisons. (Malaysia has an imprisonment rate of 141 and a murder rate of only 2.4, similar to the UK's 124 and 2.1. So does this similarity tell us anything?)

It is also interesting to look at the happy Costa Rica. With its relatively high murder rate, what's going on here?

In Table 3.5 the imprisonment and murder rankings and rates are combined. (The countries are listed alphabetically.)

Table 3.5

Country	Imprisonment world rank	Imprisonment per 100,000 population	Murder world rank	Murder rate per 100,000 population
Costa Rica	53	181	40	5.7
Denmark	121	77	108	0.8
Iceland	147	40	100	1.0
India	151	30	51	3.7
Nepal	155	26	52	3.4
Russia	2	611	8	19.9
Singapore	14	350	117	0.5
South Africa	18	335	3	47.5
South Korea	101	97	69	2.2
UK	83	124	72	2.1
US	1	738	44	5.6

This would appear to show that, apart from Singapore, there is no correlation between a high imprisonment rate and a low murder rate. Denmark and Iceland have very low rates of both. The US and Russia (especially the latter) have relatively high rates of both. South Korea has an experience rather similar to that of the UK. So if we are faced with our questioner wanting to know what the best rate of imprisonment might be, we could send them to Singapore to have a look at how at their system works. But perhaps Denmark and Iceland will also be very much worth a visit.

So where are we now? The above murder and imprisonment rates are obviously telling us very little. The fact that we ended up with a conflicting position (Singapore on the one hand; Denmark and Iceland on the other) shows us that there isn't a simple equation to use in determining the prison population's best size. This example illustrates the point well that, in decision making, we must try to eliminate any over-simplistic responses by asking questions of any evidence that is available. You will remember that we needed to ask the following question when considering decisions on early release programmes.

What is the best size for the prison population?

The answer given now turns out to be even more unsatisfactory, given our brief examination of some of the data.

The best size is whatever is needed for the number of criminals who need putting in prison.

So what is this then?

PRODUCING THE CRITERIA THAT CAN/SHOULD BE USED IN EVALUATING THE CHOICES AVAILABLE

If we return to our issue of early release from prison, then we can see that an evidence-based (rather than a literally prejudiced) approach will require us to ask questions about the issue. These questions will enable us to focus on how we should approach it.

QUESTIONS ON THE PURPOSE OF THE POLICY

Some of these questions are to do with the purpose of an early release policy. Here are some examples.

- Is it to save money?
- Is it in recognition of the good work that can be done in prisons (such that the purpose of imprisonment can be achieved early)?
- Is it to reduce overcrowding in prisons?
- Is it because of a shortage of prison staff?

Further questions are concerned with how we might evaluate an early release programme.

- Do those released early have a different risk of reoffending to those not released early? (This could be lower, higher or the same.)
- Do the early release schemes save money?
- Do they improve prisoner behaviour if early release is based at least in part on behaviour?
- Do they cause resentment with those prisoners who aren't released early (and thus cause behaviour to be worse)?

Of course, in doing such evaluation we need to ask a general question.

- Are the characteristics of those who are released early sufficiently similar to those who aren't, to be able to usefully compare the two groups in terms of outcomes on possible reoffending?

This general question should be unpacked into specific ones such as the following.

- Are the two groups sufficiently similar in age?
- Are the two groups sufficiently similar in offence(s) committed?
- Are the two groups sufficiently similar in educational level?

This question-asking method has already taken us along the route towards the next aspect of applying Critical Thinking to decision making. This is to produce criteria that can be used in evaluating any choices that have been identified.

THE MEANING OF 'CRITERIA'

What do we mean by 'criteria'? It is often ignored (or not understood) that the word 'criteria' is the plural of 'criterion' (like 'phenomena' is the plural of 'phenomenon'). Thus always avoid the mistake of referring to 'this/a criteria'. We are using the word in its conventional way as referring to 'standards by which something can be judged'. It has the same Greek origin as the word 'critic' (someone who judges) and therefore, of course, 'critical'.

GENERATING CRITERIA

If we are searching for criteria of choice, we are then looking for ways by which we make judgements about choices. If we continue with the issue of early release for the time being, we can see that our previous questions have started to generate relevant criteria.

The criteria will in part take us to consider the purpose of imprisonment. It is a familiar discussion. At least four purposes are normally identified.

- Prisons have the function of containment. They isolate and control people whose behaviour is deemed to be anti-social.
- Prisons have the function of punishment. They provide a way of making law breakers suffer in some way as a result of being deprived of their liberty.
- Prisons have the function of deterrence. They are meant to be sufficiently unappealing for most people not to want to be sent to one. It can be seen that the functions of punishment and deterrence are very much linked.
- Prisons have the function of rehabilitation. They provide the means by which those who can/will change their behaviour away from further law breaking can do so.

Prisons could, of course, provide all four functions. (They could have other functions too, such as employment – of prison officers, prison education and medical staff and so on. But these are what can be seen as hidden or indirect functions: no politician is going to justify building more prisons on the grounds of employment of prison officers, employees of building companies and so on.)

EFFECTIVENESS

Given these four functions, we can see that one way of judging a choice along the continuum is to look at the criterion of effectiveness. What do we mean by this? In this context we mean, how effective is an early release scheme in achieving its purpose? (We need to note, at this stage, that we're not doing an exercise specifically describing and evaluating the UK Government's specific early release scheme. We're just considering how we might approach an early release scheme.)

If the purpose of an early release scheme is to reduce the prison population, how effective might it be? Several issues arise here.

- Its effectiveness could be high if those released early are not recalled to prison for the breaking of one of the conditions of early release (including obviously the committal of further crimes). (And will be low if not.)
- Its effectiveness could be high if its purpose of rehabilitation works by enabling the ex-prisoner to get employment, return to their family and so on. (And will be low if not.)

- Its effectiveness could be low if prison ceases to have an appropriate punishment and thus deterrent effect. If this was the case, then the prison population could increase.

As we can see, the criterion of effectiveness requires that we are clear about the purpose(s) or outcome(s) of the decision/policy/recommendation. In this respect, it might be that there are all sorts of hidden or unexpected consequences that affect its effectiveness. For example, it could be that an unexpected consequence of an early release scheme is an increase (or a reduction) in employment in the insurance industry. This would work as follows.

The early release scheme increases the amount of property crime committed (by releasing offenders convicted of robbery/burglary/shoplifting back into the community and a significant number of them reoffend). This leads to an increase in the number of insurance claims which, in turn, leads to an increase in employment in the insurance industry. The opposite effect would have the early release prisoners reducing their level of offending (including down to none at all) because they are well supported in their community leading to fewer insurance claims and thus reduced employment.

COST

This is a very familiar criterion to use. In most decision-making tasks the cost of different choices needs to be considered. This is not to say that it is the most important criterion, although sometimes it will be. The application of this criterion also needs to be done in a way that recognises the often wider effects on cost caused by different choices. We'll see how this works in the present context.

The criterion of cost with an early release programme works in some direct ways. We would need to know the following.

- How much do prison places cost? This would need to be subdivided into the cost of different types of prison place as not all prison places cost the same – high security prisons are obviously more expensive than others. Early release schemes will take prisoners from perhaps the cheaper end but even here the costs could be considerable. The annual average cost of a prison place in the UK is at least £40,000 and at least $30,000 in the US. To create a new prison place will cost at least three times that amount.

- How much does an early release programme cost? This is very difficult to establish. It depends if there is any community support programme involved. The average cost of an individual having probation support in the UK is almost £700 per year.
- Linking back to the criterion of effectiveness, the cost of early release has to be seen in terms of the various possible outcomes. Does it save money by reducing the need to spend money on prison places? Or does it increase expenditure by lowering the deterrent effect of prisons, thus increasing offending? Does it increase expenditure by increasing policing through an increased crime rate? Does it reduce costs by getting offenders back to work and back with their families (thus reducing the need for State support of dependants)? Does it increase/reduce costs by increased/reduced reoffending leading to increased/reduced insurance costs?

The costs of early release also need to be considered in a wider way than just prison costs. We've seen one example of this with the effects on insurance. We've also referred to policing and State support for dependants. But Critical Thinking puts a great emphasis on creative thinking. So here's an example in which we need to think creatively about the possible costs. In doing this, we can come up with some aspects of cost that we wouldn't normally put into this equation.

- There is the issue of the cost of home and commercial security. If offending goes up as a result of this programme, then more needs to be spent on security systems. This is an increased cost. But it's also a benefit. More spending on security systems means more employment in companies supplying and fitting these systems. More employment means greater taxation, which means greater resources for spending on State-financed programmes (such as education, health, road-building and so on), all of which have the potential to increase employment and so... In addition, increased employment in the security industry will lead to increased demand for various things through the spending of the people employed in it. This increased demand will lead to increased income which will lead to increased tax revenues and so...
- If reoffending goes down as a result of the early release programme, then the police could focus their time on preventing further crime, thus leading to a reduced level of crime, thus lowering costs.
- If reoffending goes up as a result of the early release programme, this will lead to greater costs for those parts of the criminal justice system other than prisons. For example, the legal profession (not noted for its low level of costs) would have even more money (so leading to more demand for various

goods and services – including perhaps security systems – and thus greater tax revenues..). The security firms that transport to and from courts and prisons will have more work. And so will the companies that supply to these firms – makers of uniforms, vehicle-manufacturers, fuel-suppliers and so on.

This sort of approach is a highly productive aspect of applying Critical Thinking to a problem. We raise one point or ask one question, and all sorts of other points come out of it. We follow a sequence of thinking and allow it to take us to areas we might not have thought of initially. We can see already that when we start thinking about the cost implications of a proposal (or choice on the continuum), we end up seeing the possible implications as considerably more widespread (and indeed complex) than we had originally thought.

COST AS 'EFFECT'

In addition to this process of following a sequence of thinking, it might well be necessary to return to where we started in this chapter, and ask questions about the meaning of the word 'cost'. We have taken it to mean financial cost. But it could be taken to have the wider meaning of 'effect'. When we pay for something, it has an effect on how much money we have. But cost as 'effect' can also include a more general sense.

In this context, we can ask the question, 'What costs other than financial ones could an early release scheme have?' Here are some possible answers.

- There might be a psychological cost for victims of crime. If the person who was robbed, burgled, swindled and so on knows that the person who committed the crime has been released early, they are likely to suffer some distress as a result.
- There might be a psychological cost for the wider public as a result of the knowledge that prisoners are being released early. They might have less faith in the criminal justice system, with corresponding behaviours in terms of willingness to obey the law. This is often referred to as a type of 'social cost'.

Of course, in addition to costs as negative effect, there could be benefits of this type.

- There is likely to be a psychological benefit for the person released early.
- There might be a psychological benefit for the family of the person who has been released early. This benefit might then reinforce the positive feeling that the early released prisoner feels.

- There might be a psychological benefit for those who see early release as justified by a moral concern for the welfare of offenders.

We have seen that applying the criterion of cost to the issue of early release (whatever position on the continuum of choice it is applied to) shows all sorts of complexities. If we return to where we started with this topic, you will remember that we looked at the implied criticism of the early release of 80,000 prisoners by the UK Government. We can clarify the problem with regard to cost in the following way.

How can we measure the costs of either having an early release programme or not?

The significance of this general question can be emphasised by specific questions.

- What costs are to be included?
- Are the costs simply economic ones?

SNAPSHOT AND LONGER-TERM COSTS

But we're not finished yet. We've taken costs to mean those that can be provided in a snapshot way. By this we mean that we're looking at costs as they are incurred now.

- What is the cost of a prison place?
- What is the cost of reoffending in terms of associated costs to the criminal justice system, insurance and so on?

These snapshot costs give us something relevant but they ignore how costs might change over time. Even on a short timescale (say a year), these snapshot costs might distort the longer-term costs. Perhaps, in the longer-term, the early released prisoners might end up being more law-abiding than those who aren't released early (perhaps as a result of getting back to work earlier). Perhaps, in the longer term, not having an early release programme could be more expensive in having to build more prisons. Perhaps in the longer-term, crime could go up or down as a result of having or not having an early release programme. Here's a possible scenario.

Abandon early release scheme → need more prison places → build more prisons → courts encouraged/choose/required to fill the places, by imposing more custodial sentences → more offenders go to prison → more offenders (based on evidence that people serving short sentences have a high rate of reoffending) → need more prison places...

Given that crime has a considerable cost implication, if we don't know (or even have any idea) how an early release programme could affect crime levels, then it's difficult to see how the Critical Thinker could accept the implication that 80,000 early releases is a bad thing. At best, the Critical Thinker just keeps asking questions designed to clarify the issues.

We've looked at cost as a criterion. We'll now look at a different criterion.

PUBLIC OPINION

There are many organisations that don't have to take this criterion into account (or at least not include it as an important criterion) in their decision making. In addition, there will obviously be some countries in which this wouldn't be a relevant criterion at all. Countries that are low on the Democracy Index are obvious ones. But, because we're engaged in looking at an issue for which public opinion is seen as relevant, we'll include it as a criterion that could affect how decisions might be made.

Public opinion and Critical Thinking don't necessarily sit well together. If they did, then the use of the poster about early release would have backfired in that the public's response would have been to ask questions about the significance of the evidence. There is a lot of evidence that public opinion in various countries is poorly informed about the subject of crime. For example, it is normally based on an over-estimate of the amount of crime and it is normally far more punitive than the courts.[9]

So, with regard to making a decision about an early release programme, public opinion is likely to be relevant in terms of what is politically acceptable but not necessarily as a criterion that can improve our understanding of the issue.

OTHER CRITERIA

Other criteria for evaluating choices may be very specific to the issue being considered. For example, legality could be relevant. It clearly sits oddly as a criterion with regard to early release as this is a legal process but, with other choices, it could be more of a problem.

We'll look at some material on a topic we considered earlier to see how a range of specific criteria can operate.

We considered above the problem of definition in relation to the issue of foreign aid.

We'll now return to this issue. If we were to look at foreign aid in terms of a continuum of choice, then there would be entries such as:

- increase the level of aid to all countries with a GDP lower than $x.
- Ensure that all countries with a GDP higher than $x pay a minimum of y% of their GDP.
- Reduce the level of aid to those countries which score below 2.0 on the democracy index.
- Place specified conditions on the receipt of aid.
- Withdraw aid to those countries which are engaged in civil war.
- Withdraw aid to those countries which score highly (specified) on measures of corruption.

You can see that such a continuum would be a very long one. Of course, for most purposes, we would not need to produce a continuum that includes every option as presumably we would already have limited its range.

So what specific criteria would this issue of aid involve? We could use the following.

- The nature of the political regime.
- The extent of need in each country.
- The cause of the need for foreign aid.
- The way in which any aid has been used in the past.

THE NATURE OF THE POLITICAL REGIME

This is a very important criterion that is often overlooked in relation to the subject of aid. Do we treat all countries in the same way?

The example of Robert Mugabe is a useful one. He is well known for his suppression of dissent in Zimbabwe, and also for presiding over the rapid decline of the Zimbabwean economy, turning a once prosperous country into one with huge problems of malnourishment. His government has destroyed the temporary shelters that many city-living people had built, forcing them into a life of extreme poverty. Would this be relevant in determining whether aid should be provided? If so, how would it affect the level of aid?

There is also the example of Sudan. In March 2009, the International Criminal Court (ICC) issued an arrest warrant for President Bashir of Sudan for playing an 'essential role' in the murder, rape, torture, pillaging and displacement of a large number of people in Darfur in Sudan. Half an hour after the ICC ordered the arrest of President Bashir, the Sudanese regime ordered 13 aid agencies to leave the country immediately.[10] Oxfam lost £5 million and Médecins sans Frontières lost £1.7 million (with neither able to get this back).

A recently published book with the powerful title *Dead Aid* has argued that aid can make the quality of the government of the aided country worse, so increasing the poverty of the country.[11] This works, it is argued, in the same way as large oil revenues can reduce the accountability of governments. Quite simply, foreign aid can keep bad regimes in power by enabling them to continue without any useful concern about public welfare.

A different (although probably related) issue that might be relevant here is the extent of corruption in different countries. Should we use this evidence to argue that the nature of the regime is significant in deciding what to do about aid?

Tables 3.6 and 3.7 draw on figures published by the annual Corruption Perceptions Index.[12] This ranks countries according to how much corruption is perceived to exist among politicians and public officials by business people, academics and risk analysts. The score ranges from 0 to 10, with 10 being the least corrupt. Some of the countries we met above appear at either end of the index. (Some figures are included for those that are least corrupt for interest rather than for analysis, although you might want to consider doing this.)

Table 3.6 Lowest corruption scores (ranked from the least corrupt), 2008

Rank	Country	Score
1 =	Denmark	9.3
1 =	New Zealand	9.3
1 =	Sweden	9.3
4	Singapore	9.2
5 =	Finland	9.0
5 =	Switzerland	9.0
7	Iceland	8.9
12	Hong Kong	8.1
16	UK	7.7

Table 3.7 Highest corruption scores (ranked from the most corrupt), 2008

Rank	Country	Score
1	Somalia	1.0
2 =	Myanmar	1.3
4	Haiti	1.4
6 =	Chad	1.6
6 =	Sudan	1.6
9	Congo-Kinshasa	1.7
13	Togo	2.7
14 =	Malawi	2.8
14 =	Zambia	2.8

If we take the degree of corruption as evidence of the nature of the political regime, then this criterion could be used to question whether any aid should be sent to countries like Somalia, Myanmar and Sudan.

A survey of public attitudes to the 2005 'Make Poverty History' campaign can provide us with further useful evidence here.[13] The results of the survey showed that many people saw the nature of the regime as a problem. For example, 79% of the respondents saw 'corrupt and incompetent African governments' as one of the factors that 'have contributed most to Africa's problems'.

The survey evidence also gave support for the idea that help should not be given indiscriminately. One of the survey questions raised the issue of corruption and showed that 83% were either 'not very confident' or 'not at all confident' that money given wouldn't end up in 'the pockets of criminals and corrupt governments.'

THE EXTENT OF NEED IN EACH COUNTRY

This is another specific criterion that could be relevant to this issue.

There is a variation on using GDP per head as the basis of establishing need in a country. This is to use what is called 'Purchasing Power Parity' or PPP. This statistic is useful because it adjusts for cost of living differences in calculating the price of a standard 'basket' of goods and services. PPP estimates are often given as an index with the US counting as 100.

Table 3.8 Countries with lowest purchasing power, 2007[14]

Rank	Country	PPP
1	Zimbabwe	0.4
2 =	Burundi	0.7
2 =	Congo-Kinshasa	0.7
4	Liberia	0.8
7	Somalia	1.3
8 =	Niger	1.4
10 =	Sierra Leone	1.5
13 =	Malawi	1.7
13 =	Togo	1.7
16	Mozambique	1.8
17 =	Myanmar	1.9
17 =	Rwanda	1.9

The evidence on PPP amongst the poorest countries of the world shows that on this list there are, perhaps not surprisingly, countries that we have met in other evidence that we have looked at. A comparison with the corruption index shows that there are some countries that appear on both of these lists. Here we have a problem for decision making in that we have a possible conflict between criteria. How should we deal with a country like Somalia, with its high levels of need and very widespread corruption?[15]

There is another point about need. You might have seen that it's often claimed that developed countries ought to pay at least 0.7% of their Gross National Income (GNI) in foreign aid. (GNI is a country's GDP together with any income received from other countries in rent, interest and so on, minus any such payments paid to other countries.) The study *The Ghost of 0.7*[16] shows that this was taken as an entirely arbitrary figure, with no useful thinking behind it. In addition, the authors of the study make the point that it is a strange idea to take the size of a country's GNI as the factor that determines how much undeveloped countries should get. In one important sense, it could be argued that undeveloped countries need £x rather than 0.7% of the GNI of rich countries. It is perhaps rather like you or me going to our bank and pointing out that, given the size of their wealth, we should have a certain percentage of it rather than how much we need. (Try it and see what they say.)

Of course, as Critical Thinkers, we might want to say that the criterion of 'need' raises all sorts of definitional questions. What do we mean by 'need'? Looking at

PPP was not without merit in that it gives us an indication of what people in a country can buy. It doesn't require much imagination to appreciate something of the massive contrast between a person's life in Zimbabwe with its PPP of 0.4 and that in Luxembourg with the highest figure of 174.3 (or Singapore on 109.0). But need might be met in other ways. It could be, for example, that a country with a low PPP has a very good health care or education system, thus benefiting its people in ways not measured by PPP.

There is another measure that can be used. This is the Human Development Index (HDI). This includes income levels, degree of adult literacy, life expectancy and average years of schooling. It is given on a scale from 0 to 100.

Which countries are the top ones? We meet again some very familiar ones: Iceland (top with a score of 96.8), Norway, Canada, Australia, Ireland, the Netherlands, Sweden, Japan, Luxembourg, France, Switzerland, Finland and Denmark.

Which countries are at the bottom? Again, there are some, by now, familiar ones: Sierra Leone (bottom with a score of 32.9), Central African Republic, Congo-Kinshasa, Liberia, Mozambique, Niger, Burkina Faso, Burundi, Rwanda and Malawi are all in the bottom 18.

Sierra Leone could be said, then, to be the country with the greatest need. On this basis, if need is a determining criterion in making decisions, foreign aid should certainly be sent there. Following the civil war in this country, a massive amount of foreign aid was sent there, but it is only 18th in the league table for recipients of aid in $ per head (with $92.3). Top of this league table is the West Bank and Gaza with a staggering $479 per head. So, if we take the HDI as the most reliable guide to need, then need is not the most important criterion in actual decision making with regard to foreign aid. (We should, of course, look at the value of a $ in Sierra Leone. You will have seen above in Table 3.8, which shows countries with the lowest purchasing power, that Sierra Leone is 10th, with a PPP of only 1.5.)

THE CAUSE OF THE NEED FOR FOREIGN AID

This is another specific criterion that could be relevant. For example, countries in which life expectancy is low are very likely to find it difficult to develop economically. They will not have the labour force necessary to do so. Zimbabwe has the lowest male life expectancy (43.4 years) and the second lowest female life expectancy (44.3 years).

Another source of evidence could be rates of corruption. Perhaps funding for important economic development was siphoned off by corrupt politicians and/or public officials. This could then lead to the country having to borrow more or to making it difficult to repay loans because of failed economic projects (or both).

Another problem could be a civil war. This would have all sorts of economic (as well as humanitarian) consequences. For example, the civil war in Sierra Leone left thousands mutilated by the rebels' practice of cutting off civilians' hands and legs.

THE WAY IN WHICH ANY AID HAS BEEN USED IN THE PAST

This could be seen as a sub-category of the previous criterion, in that the need for aid might be a consequence of how it was mis-spent in the past.

Some of the money might have been used for projects that don't help the general population (such as the lavish spending by the King of Swaziland on sumptuous palaces and expensive cars, including 20 Mercedes and a new Rolls Royce in 2010). Perhaps we would want to look at the levels of military expenditure. For example, as we saw above, Burundi had the second-lowest PPP in the world (and the lowest GDP) but is 11th out of 173 for military spending as a percentage of GDP. (Sierra Leone is 73rd; Costa Rica, by the way, is 164th; and Iceland is 173rd.) However, there might be very good reasons why a country needs to spend a high proportion of its GDP (even though the GDP is low) on its military. It could be that it needs to prevent civil war from breaking out again (as with Sierra Leone and Burundi).

It could be useful to make an analogy here with individuals who are in debt. If an individual is in debt because she was made redundant and, despite her best endeavours, can't get a job, we would presumably be sympathetic to her being helped. If another individual is in debt because she has spent her substantial lottery winnings on a whirl of flash holidays, cars and handbags, then we would (presumably) be less sympathetic to helping her.

Is this analogy relevant? If it is, is the evidence on the King of Swaziland relevant here? Does this evidence enable us to make the use of aid an important criterion? It would be difficult to see how the use of aid could be seen as irrelevant to decision making on this subject.

PULLING THINGS TOGETHER

You might have been thinking that the four specific criteria that we've been looking at in this section can be usefully seen as contextualising the general criterion of effectiveness. If we ask the question 'how effective might foreign aid be?' then the answer should address the issues of the nature of the political regime, the extent of the need, the causes of the economic problems, and how aid has been used in the past.

This is a good way of seeing the specific criteria. They are a way of unpacking the general criteria to fit the specific context. But we could go further. The specific criteria could themselves be further unpacked with regard to the specific context. Thus the specific criterion of the cause of the need for foreign aid could be unpacked into:

- historical causes
- geographical causes
- economic causes
- political regime issues

All of these could all come together to create major problems. As Professor Paul Collier has put it, 'African societies face problems deeper than their dependence on aid. Divided by ethnic loyalties, they are too large to be nations. Yet with only tiny economies, they lack the scale to be effective states. As a result the vital public goods of security and accountability cannot adequately be provided. In their absence the valuable natural assets that many countries possess become liabilities instead of opportunities for prosperity.'[17]

DECISION MAKING: FROM CLARITY TO CONTINUA TO CRITERIA

We're going to return to some of these issues in the next chapter but, first, it would be useful to look at what we've done so far.

In a decision-making task, we will normally begin with a question that needs to be answered. In the examples we've looked at, we had these questions.

- What shall we do about the issue of early release?
- What shall we do about the issue of foreign aid?

The procedure that we then used can be seen like this. You will see that it has a wonderful tree-like appearance (although it's an upside-down tree!). This fits well with what's going on. At each stage, there is some growth built on what's been developed before.

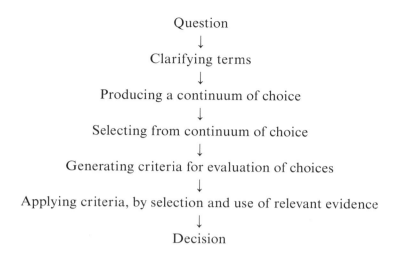

Question
↓
Clarifying terms
↓
Producing a continuum of choice
↓
Selecting from continuum of choice
↓
Generating criteria for evaluation of choices
↓
Applying criteria, by selection and use of relevant evidence
↓
Decision

Though the process shows that a decision was made, we need to revisit the process to look more at what's going on.

NOTES

1. Yale University Press, 1980. For a discussion of some of the points raised in the book and a critical evaluation of them, see my 'Liberal Dialogue, Citizenship and Mentally Handicapped Persons', *Political Studies*, 1986, xxiv, 374–86.
2. R. Veenhoven, 'Average happiness in 148 nations 2000–09, World Database of Happiness'. Rankreport Average Happiness, version 10/09. http://worlddatabaseofhappiness.eur.nl
3. However, John Keble's words for the hymn, 'The daily round, the common task, should furnish all we ought to ask, room to deny ourselves...' very much suggest that we should aim for rather minimal satisfaction.
4. Source of statistics for population size and GDP: *Pocket World in Figures*. Profile Books, 2010.
5. www.economist.com/media/pdf/democracy_index_2007
6. See my *Critical Thinking for A2*. How To Books, 2006. Chapter 2.
7. Source of statistics: United Nations Development Programme, 2007, www.allcountries.org/ranks/prison_incarceration_rates_of_countries_2007.html
8. Source of statistics: United Nations Development Programme, 2000–04, www.photius.com/rankings/murder_rate_of_countries_2000-2004.html
9. See, for example, www.esc-eurocrim.org/files/summary.pdf
10. L. Polman, *War Games: The Story of Aid and War in Modern Times*. Viking, 2010.
11. D. Moyo, *Dead Aid*. Penguin, 2010.
12. *Pocket World in Figures*. Profile Books, 2010. p. 65.

13. YouGov/Daily Telegraph Survey on Africa, YouGov plc, 2005.
14. *Pocket World in Figures*. Profile Books, 2010. p. 29.
15. See the debate on whether foreign intervention is justified in Somalia on www.economist.com of June 2010. (The motion that 'foreigners should intervene in Somalia' was carried by 55% for to 45% against.)
16. M. Clemens and T. Moss, *The Ghost of 0.7%*, International Policy Network, 2010.
17. P. Collier, review of *Dead Aid*, *Independent*, 30 January 2009.

4

DECISION MAKING – RELEVANCE, INFERENCES AND CONSEQUENCES

WHAT IS RELEVANCE?

In Chapter 1, we raised questions about the issue of relevance when we were considering the significance of claims in the argument against longlining. In Chapter 3, we spent some time developing a method for decision making by producing choices and criteria to evaluate these choices. In applying criteria, we made frequent use of statistical and other evidence. For example, you will remember that we used measures like GDP, PPP and Happy Life Years.

But in the previous chapter we passed by a question without especially noticing it. This question is hanging around waiting to be answered, like a guest at the door. It's a question we don't always notice (because we don't think about the need to answer it) but it's probably best that we deal with this guest at the door because, as we'll see, it's not going to go away in any serious account of Critical Thinking. The question is:

What is relevance?

Is the evidence in the following argument relevant to the inference?

A 2009 survey showed that 69% of the population of the European Union (EU) believe that poverty, lack of food and drinking water are among the most serious problems facing the world as a whole. So the EU should do all that it can to deal with these problems.

The answer to this question about relevance depends in this example on the meaning of the inference. Is it that 'the EU should do all that it can' because it has a duty to respond to the wishes of the people in the EU? Is it because the people of the EU are correct in identifying these problems as 'among the most serious . . . facing the world'? Is it because the problem is going to affect the EU? Or what?

This argument, as you will have seen, relies on an appeal to popularity. You will remember that in Chapter 1 we looked at how claims have a neutral significance until something is done with them. As in the short argument above, the claim about the 69% cent of people in the EU has no significance until the inference is drawn from it. Inference, we noted, is the process of extracting imputed significance from a claim. So we could use the evidence very differently.

> A 2009 survey showed that 69% of the population of the European Union believe that poverty, lack of food and drinking water are among the most serious problems facing the world as a whole. So the EU should develop policies to reduce the world's population. / So the EU should ensure that these problems are solved for the countries of the EU. / . . .

You will probably have noticed that we're back to where we were in the latter part of Chapter 1. Whereas in deductive arguments, the appropriate inference is determined entirely by the premises, in inductive arguments we have a range of possible inferences rather than just one. The key to the limits on this range is centrally that of relevance.

We addressed some features of relevance in that chapter by looking at the issue of connectivity. But there is still more work to be done on connectivity and relevance. Though it might seem obvious whether a claim is relevant or irrelevant to an inference, it is in fact less straightforward.

RELEVANCE – AN EXAMPLE: ALCOHOL ADVERTISING

Let's look at another example.

> In the UK, advertising of alcoholic drinks is a significant contributor to the increase in the number of young people who drink. This significant role of adverts in creating drinkers can be seen when one looks at how the drinking habits of young people have changed. In the 1920s and 1930s the 18–24 age group had the lowest consumption of alcohol in the adult population and were the group most likely not to drink. By the 1980s, the picture was exactly the opposite. It is no surprise that alcohol advertising did not target the young in the 1920s and 1930s. In fact, the relationship between advertising and

consumption can be shown even more clearly. When we look at the figures for expenditure on alcohol advertising from 1992–2000 and those for the amount of alcohol consumption by 11–15 year olds during the same period, we find that the level of increase in the two is exactly the same year by year.

As you can see, the author's inference that advertising creates young drinkers is drawn from four (or, as we'll see, really five) evidence-claims. In addition, one of these ('By the 1980s, the picture was exactly the opposite.') requires an assumed additional piece of evidence – advertising was targeting the 18–24 age group in the 1980s.

But are any of the evidence-claims relevant? Let's look at the fourth. It is, in effect, two claims: alcohol advertising went up by x during 1992–2000; alcohol consumption by 11–15 year olds went up by x during the same time. The two claims are seen as acting together but, in acting together, they are being used as an independent evidence-claim (thus not dependent for their significance on any of the others). So is this claim relevant to the inference?

The problem with the relevance of this claim is that it could be used in support of three different inferences.

Alcohol advertising went up by x during 1992–2000; alcohol consumption by 11–15 year olds went up by x during the same time → alcohol advertising causes 11–15 year olds to drink / an increase in 11–15 year olds drinking caused drinks companies to advertise more / alcohol advertising both causes 11–15 year olds to drink and is caused by their drinking.

Furthermore, you will probably have noted that the evidence-claim need not support any of these inferences in that the relationship between them could be coincidental. This would produce the following argument.

Though alcohol advertising went up by x during 1992–2000 and alcohol consumption by 11–15 year olds went up by x during the same time, there is no causal link between the two because there are explanations for each which do not require the other.

TESTS FOR RELEVANCE

MAKING A DIFFERENCE

Here then we have a problem! How can an evidence-claim be relevant to contradictory inferences? In her book *Critical Reasoning*, Anne Thomson suggests that the way in which we should look for relevance is to ask if it 'makes a difference' to the acceptability of the conclusion.[1] This has an appeal but it doesn't nail down what we want. Let's suppose we can show that the reason(s) for the increase in 11–15 year-olds drinking wasn't/weren't anything to do with advertising, then this evidence-claim is irrelevant to an inference that it was. It made a difference, but only in an illusory way. This illusory character of relevance is shown clearly in the next argument.

> Every day we can see that the sun appears in different parts of the sky, such that at dawn it appears in the east and at dusk it appears in the west. This movement of the sun across the sky shows us that it is indeed the sun rather than the Earth that is moving.

In this example, the evidence of our senses is used to draw an inference that we know to be straightforwardly wrong. The simple point is that the evidence from our senses is in this case entirely irrelevant. The test 'Does it make a difference?' doesn't help here at all.

Here's another example.

> Anaxagoras split open a deformed ram's skull to prove that its single horn was a freak of nature and not, as a rival philosopher claimed, an augury favourable to Pericles. The people were impressed at first, but suspended their admiration when Pericles came to power.[2]

Here we have a piece of evidence being interpreted by people as relevant to an explanation for Pericles (a famous Athenian statesman and general) coming to power. Anaxagoras (a notable Greek philosopher and scientist) got it right but his explanation was seen as irrelevant. So asking the question, 'Does the ram's deformed horn make a difference to a prediction that Pericles would come to power?' gives us the right answer with Anaxagoras and the wrong one with the other philosopher. We know that the ram's deformed horn was simply, straightforwardly irrelevant to a prediction about Pericles, though it made a difference.

WEAKENING CONNECTIVITY

We can make progress with nailing down relevance by returning to what in Chapter 1 we referred to as 'connectivity'. You will remember that we used this term to point to the degree to which an inference was connected to a claim or to claims. This focused us again on the issue of the significance which an inference gives to the claim(s). This connectivity can be weakened in various ways.

- With evidence-claims, it is weakened by there being at least one other plausible (reasonable) explanation which would give the claim a different significance.

- With principle-claims, it is weakened by there being an alternative principle.

- With prediction-claims, it is weakened by there being disputable evidence-claims and questionable claims/assumptions about the future timescale.

- With the use of analogies and disanalogies, it is weakened by differences and similarities respectively between the situations.

RELEVANCE AND CONNECTIVITY

In this way, we can see relevance (and, obviously, irrelevance) in terms of the degree to which a claim has connectivity with an inference. This focuses us better than 'making a difference' in that it looks at what the inference requires of the claim(s) in terms of whether the significance it gives to the claim(s) is non-problematic. Relevance requires that we start with an inference or at least some idea of what sort of inference we might be looking at.

Let's look again at some more of the passage on advertising and drinking.

> In the 1920s and 1930s the 18–24 age group had the lowest consumption of alcohol in the adult population and were the group most likely not to drink. By the 1980s, the picture was exactly the opposite. It is no surprise that alcohol advertising did not target the young in the 1920s and 1930s.

So, using connectivity as our method, is any of this evidence relevant? You'll remember that the inference was this.

> In the UK, advertising of alcoholic drinks is a significant contributor to the increase in the number of young people who drink.

What does this require to be drawn? It obviously requires evidence which points to a causal relationship between advertising and young people drinking. But it requires evidence for which there is no plausible alternative explanation, otherwise the inference will be insufficiently connected with the claim.

The evidence that is presented has many problems.

- The author assumes that alcohol advertising did target the 18–24 age group by the 1980s. No evidence is provided for this.

- The author assumes that there are no explanations other than the lack of targeted advertising for the low levels of alcohol consumption by the 18–24 age group in the 1920s and 1930s. There might be such alternative explanations.

- The author assumes that there are no explanations other than advertising for the change in drinking habits by the 18–24 age group by the 1980s. There might be such alternative explanations.

- The author fails to provide evidence on alcohol consumption by the 18–24 age group between the 1940s and the 1970s.

Similar points could be made about the earlier evidence on the 11–15 year olds.

- The evidence on advertising and consumption by 11–15 year olds between 1992 and 2000 could be no more than coincidence. (Again we could find plausible alternative explanations for the increase in drinking.)

- The growth in advertising and consumption by 11–15 year olds between 1992 and 2000 needs to be considered in the light of the initial levels of each, otherwise numerical comparisons will be misleading.

So is all this evidence relevant? Does it provide a useful degree of connectivity to the inference? No, not really. The author has failed to show the relevance of this evidence in that there are other explanations for it that would provide a different significance. Quite simply, as it stands, the evidence doesn't, in Thomson's words, 'make a difference'.

THE FATAL FLAW IN THE 'MAKING A DIFFERENCE' TEST FOR RELEVANCE

What we can see is that 'making a difference' is a criterion that is fatally flawed by circularity. When we ask, 'Is x relevant?' and we're given the answer, 'Yes, if it makes a difference', we doing no more than going in a circle. To see why, just reverse the sequence. 'Does x make a difference?' produces the answer, 'Yes, if it's relevant'. In other words, then, the answer to the question, 'Is x relevant?' becomes 'Yes, if x is relevant'.

After all this, it might be useful to make a distinction between different types of relevance. We can talk about 'preliminary relevance' and 'established relevance'. This will mean that claims that look as if they might contribute to connectivity with an inference can be accepted as having a preliminary relevance. If this connectivity can be shown to be present, then we can change the status of the claim to that of 'established relevance'.

But before we leave this discussion of the problem of relevance, we need to show why, in addition, beyond circularity, Thomson's measure of 'Does it make a difference?' simply won't do the work that we want it to do. It won't do this because it doesn't successfully distinguish between relevance and irrelevance. It allows someone to claim something as relevant when it's not. Look at the next example.

> Richard Branson has claimed that his mother was an important factor in his becoming a highly successful entrepreneur. It's obvious then that budding entrepreneurs should ask their mother to be their business mentor.

Is the Richard Branson example relevant? Does it make a difference to the inference? In a very important way, the answer is 'No, it doesn't'. We wouldn't normally allow a generalisation from just one example. Of course, some people might object, pointing out that, since Branson is a hugely successful entrepreneur, his experience should be able to be generalised. But presumably we could find successful entrepreneurs who would not rate their mother as being significant in their success. All we would have done is countered one example with another. So, importantly, we would say that the Richard Branson example hasn't even got a preliminary relevance even though some might want to say that it made a difference.

THE STRONG TEST FOR RELEVANCE

Critical Thinking has to earn its keep by, at the very least, providing guidelines for the evaluation of reasoning. Such guidelines have to be helpful in as many situations as possible. So when our man in the street comes along and uses the Branson example, we can't simply ask, 'Does it make a difference?', because he might say 'Yes'. Our task is then to show him why this test isn't helpful. We can show him these guidelines.

- A claim isn't relevant if it can be countered easily by another claim.

- A claim isn't relevant if it is based on research which is highly questionable (methodologically weak).

- A claim isn't relevant if it comes from a source whose authority/significance we have good reasons to question.

- A claim isn't relevant if it has been successfully challenged by a source whose authority/significance we have good reasons to accept.

- A claim isn't relevant if it has been superseded by more recent (acceptable) evidence.

- A claim isn't relevant if it deals with an issue which is significantly different from that which is being argued for or against.

- A claim isn't relevant if there are acceptable alternative explanations for the significance of any evidence used.

This last point is the one that we developed earlier (and illustrated by the reference to the evidence on alcohol consumption and advertising).

FROM IRRELEVANCE TO PRELIMINARY TO ESTABLISHED RELEVANCE

Of course, a claim might be moved from irrelevance to preliminary relevance if it can be shown, for example, that other claims support it. There will come, then, a tipping point at which we can suggest that we are dealing with relevance (even established relevance). This was illustrated well by our discussion of the additional claims in the albatross argument in Chapter 1.

These guidelines can be objected to on the basis that our uncritically thinking man in the street would simply reject them as not applying to his claim. This is an entirely understandable objection but, in response, we would have to say that Critical Thinking can't always convert prejudice into insight. But we have to, at least, try. Though the Thomson Test of difference-making will merely serve to confirm prejudice, these suggested guidelines will hopefully turn some of it into insight.

One further way of thinking about the role of these guidelines is to use again the image of an unfamiliar caller at the door. Someone calls at your door, hoping to be allowed in. If you don't know them, you would expect them to give some information about themselves. If their answers are satisfactory, you'll let them in. Those who don't give satisfactory answers are turned away. Our welcomed guests are relevance; those that are turned away are irrelevance. Our guidelines are, in this way, like the stern security staff at the door. Round the corner at the Thomson party, all sorts of undesirables are let in because security is very lax.

On this basis, then, we can return to where we began this chapter. Was the use of the evidence on GDP, PPP and Happy Life Years relevant to decision making on foreign aid? By all of the guidelines that we used, indeed it was.

This is not to say that there wasn't other evidence that should have been used. For example, we might have wanted to look at military spending as a percentage of GDP and the Global Gender Gap Index, which measures the differences between males and females in a combined score for employment, educational attainment and political representation. (Our old friends Norway, Finland, Sweden and Iceland take the first four places in this list by having the smallest gender gaps.)

RELEVANCE, DECISION MAKING AND EVIDENCE

But this question of the relevance of evidence has opened up another problematic area. How far can we go in decision making with evidence? Even if we're able to answer the question of which evidence is relevant, we're now faced with this other question. Can evidence be enough to enable us to make a decision? Before we seek to develop an answer to this question, we'll look at an example.

EVIDENCE ON TB IN BADGERS AND CATTLE

In 2007, a report was presented to the UK Government on the problem of cattle contracting tuberculosis (TB) from badgers.[3] The author, Sir David King, presented his task as to consider 'whether the removal (killing) of badgers in areas of high TB prevalence might (or might not) prevent or reduce the incidence of TB in cattle'. You will have noted the rather helpful clarification of the term 'removal' as meaning 'killing'. Apart from this clarification in paragraph 3 of the report, only the word 'removal' is given elsewhere.

King argues that 'decisions...need to be taken on badger removal in the light of the existing scientific evidence, in spite of its uncertainties'. He concludes that the evidence shows that 'badgers are a clear source of infection for cattle' and that 'removal of badgers is the best option available at the moment to reduce the reservoir of infection in wildlife'. However, the evidence also showed that, when testing for cattle TB was suspended in 2001, the amount of TB in badgers 'increased substantially'. This showed that, though badgers appear to infect cattle, cattle also appear to infect badgers.

A decision based on this evidence might lead to an argument for the 'removal' of badgers, but it could also be used to support an argument for the vaccination of cattle, greater separation between cattle and badgers, the vaccination of badgers, or for a combination of approaches (including the 'removal' of cattle).

So the evidence takes us only so far. It comes up against one important blockage: 'the overriding aim is to control TB in cattle'. Thus the position that perhaps the number of cattle should be reduced in order to reduce the risk of badgers getting TB is not considered. In this way, the evidence isn't allowed to go where it might have led us. Clearly, someone who is a great fan of badgers would start from a different position from Sir David King and would therefore allow the evidence to do different things.

We have seen how an evidence-claim gains an imputed significance when an inference is drawn from it. Thus, when we are faced with such claims, we can do one of two things.

- We can use the evidence to support an existing inference (position).

- We can see if the evidence takes us towards a possible inference (position) (or a range of possible positions).

The first of these is commonly used. You will remember that Sir David King didn't start from the position of just letting the evidence take him where it seemed to go. He started from the position of looking to see if killing badgers could reduce TB in cattle (not whether reducing the number of cattle could reduce the amount of TB in badgers). It might seem a small point but it's of considerable importance, because one possible inference was ruled out even before the evidence was looked at.

LOOKING FOR CORRELATIONS AND INFERENCE

So let's look at some evidence and see if it can take us somewhere, perhaps somewhere unexpected. We'll do this in the spirit of creativity, one of the essential features of successful Critical Thinking. We'll put together some different evidence, which perhaps wouldn't normally be put together, and see what happens.

ALCOHOL CONSUMPTION AND OTHER STATISTICS

If we were to look at the world ranking of alcohol consumption, what inference might we expect to be able to find evidence for? In Table 4.1, we have the top ten countries for alcohol consumption together with other evidence about these countries.

Table 4.1[4]

Country	Alcohol consumption*	Environmental performance index (EPI)**	Human development index (HDI)***
Germany	1	13	22
Czech Republic	2	68	32
Finland	3	4	11
Denmark	4	26	14
Russia	5	28	67
Austria	6	6	15
Venezuela	7	45	74
Poland	8	43	37
Slovakia	9	17	42
Netherlands	10	55	9

* Retail sales, litres per head of population
** Environmental Performance Index, 2008. This is a measure of the performance on a set of environmental goals, such as pollution, adequate sanitation, drinking water, biodiversity and natural resources.
*** Human Development Index, see Chapter 3

So, if we are prepared to follow evidence where it might go and see what inference could be drawn when we get there, does this table go anywhere? It's difficult to see if it does, but we could pick these points out.

- Three of the top ten countries for alcohol consumption are also in the top 25 for both EPI and HDI.
- Four of the top ten for alcohol consumption are also in the top 20 for EPI.
- Four of the top ten for alcohol consumption are also in the top 20 for HDI.
- Two of the top ten for alcohol consumption are also in the top ten for EPI.

But is the evidence taking us anywhere, such that an inference is being suggested? Probably not. So perhaps there isn't a pattern with any useful inference-suggesting correlations. Perhaps we simply haven't got enough evidence. Perhaps a possible pattern needs more evidence to reveal itself.

Here are the next ten countries in the alcohol league table (see Table 4.2).

Table 4.2

Country	Alcohol consumption	Environmental performance index (EPI)	Human development index (HDI)
Romania	11	83	60
Hungary	12	23	36
Australia	13	46	3
Ireland	14	35	5
UK	15	14	16
Belgium	16	57	17
Ukraine	17	76	76
Sweden	18	3	6
Switzerland	19	1	7
US	20	39	12

What can we now see?

- Six of the top 20 countries for alcohol consumption are also in the top 25 for both EPI and HDI.
- Seven of the top 20 for alcohol consumption are also in the top 20 for EPI.
- Eight of the top 20 for alcohol consumption are also in the top 20 for HDI.
- Four of the top 20 for alcohol consumption are also in the top ten for EPI.

Perhaps something can be glimpsed here. Though there is no obvious direct correspondence between alcohol consumption and HDI (and why should there be?), it would appear that there is something of a correlation. There are 159 countries in the HDI, so the top 20% would be those in the range 1–32. If we use this measure, then 13 out of the top 20 countries for alcohol consumption are in the top 20% for HDI – a pattern perhaps? If we do the same with EPI (149 countries), then the top 20% would give us the range 1–30. With this, we find 9 out of the top 20 for alcohol consumption in the top 20% for EPI.

A possible inference at last.

> The level of alcohol consumption in a country is a possible predictor of its HDI level (or vice versa).

Of course, we might want to find different inferences. We might want to see if there are correlations that are suggested by other evidence.

Though the HDI includes life expectancy, this measure is only one of three. So perhaps we want to see how the measures of life expectancy and alcohol consumption correlate (without interference from the other two components of HDI: educational attainment and income).

The top 20 countries for life expectancy include only five countries from the top 20 for alcohol consumption (Switzerland, Australia, Sweden, Austria and the Netherlands). To put it another way, 15 of the countries with the highest life expectancy are not in the top 20 for alcohol consumption. (If we look at specific types of alcohol consumption we have interesting variations. For example, Singapore is the eleventh highest consumer of champagne, the fourth highest importer of Scotch whisky – despite its small population – and has the seventeenth best life expectancy in the world.)

So have we another possible inference?

> The level of life expectancy in a country can possibly be predicted by its level of alcohol consumption.

This will, of course, work only within certain frameworks. Countries with high levels of alcohol consumption are developed countries, so the relatively high life expectancies could be explained in this way. As a result, the level of alcohol consumption becomes something of a red herring.

However, if we look at deaths from cancer, then only five of the top 20 countries for alcohol consumption are in the top 20 countries for such deaths (Czech Republic, Denmark, Poland, Slovakia and Hungary).

All this has shown us that sometimes evidence can point the way towards the general (even, at times, specific) direction of an inference (whether this be a recommendation, a decision, a proposal or a position). Other times, the evidence can take us nowhere because we're looking at the wrong evidence, inaccurate evidence or insufficient evidence. And then, of course, we're back to relevance.

But this sort of analysis might well encourage us to look for 'third' factors as being possibly relevant. For example, we could look again at the inference drawn earlier.

> The level of alcohol consumption in a country is a possible predictor of its HDI level (or vice versa).

In looking at this inference, we could investigate explanatory links such as society's amount of leisure, the levels of social interaction and so on. As an example of 'third' factors, there's an intriguing correlation between a common parasite and neurotic behaviour. The parasite is toxoplasma (closely related to the malaria-causing plasmodium) and can cause behavioural changes. National surveys on neuroticism have shown that people in the UK have a very low score for neuroticism (-0.8), whereas the French have a high figure of 1.8. There could well be all sorts of causes for this difference (historical, cultural and so on). However evidence has shown that 45% of French people are infected by the toxoplasma parasite whereas only 6.6% of people in the UK have this infection.[5] Is this a significant (the significant?) third factor?

So let's consider where we are now. We've clarified problematic language; we've identified a range of choices along a continuum; we've established some criteria to apply to the choices; we've considered how to judge what evidence might be relevant in applying the criteria. Having got this far, it might well be that the nature of the possible decisions that are available is getting clearer. Perhaps there are some possible decisions that are still worth looking at.

DILEMMAS

THE NATURE OF A DILEMMA

In some accounts of decision making in a Critical Thinking context, the next step is very often to reduce these decisions to just two. In doing this, you might be looking at framing these two decisions into a dilemma. This is a term which is used in everyday speech to mean something like 'being faced with a difficult situation or problem'. But in Critical Thinking it has a more focused meaning to refer to a situation in which a choice has to be made between two alternatives, each of which has a consequence or consequences which are problematic. This problematic nature of the consequences can consist in their being both undesirable and desirable, although in most cases it would be the former.

We have no reason to restrict ourselves to dilemmas, in that decision making can produce far more than two options that need consideration. (Technically, we can have trilemmas for when there's three such choices.) But we'll just have a look at these before we move on.

There is a children's book called *Would you rather?*[6] which provides lots of such dilemmas. The reader is given many options to choose from, each of which has a problem (often a big one). (Examples include the two options of either spider stew or slug dumplings, and being lost at sea and lost in the desert.)

Very compelling dilemmas include choosing between lying or betraying someone (by, for example, telling the truth about their whereabouts, such that they would suffer). Being under torture faced with this choice would be an extreme example.[7] Another extreme dilemma would be that faced by people adrift in a boat when the survival of many of them would require the death of some (so who should die?). Of course, in every case, the answer is likely to be 'Neither, thank you'.

EXAMPLES OF DILEMMAS

An obvious feature of a dilemma, then, is a choice between two options. It is also a difficult choice. Shall I buy this birthday card or that one is a choice between at least two options. It might even be seen as being difficult, although the difficulty is at a fairly low level. A 2006 publicity leaflet from Oxfam asks the question, 'What was the last dilemma you faced?' and gives examples such as, 'Stay in, go out?' They do this in order to show that such daily 'dilemmas' aren't that serious. The purpose is to contrast our easy lives with those of many people in developing countries. The example given by Oxfam emphasises the difference between many of our dilemmas and theirs. It concerns Misgane Chloe in Ethiopia.

'I had two options for drinking water. If I was tired I would fetch the water three hours away, but this was not clean. If I had more energy I would go and fetch the cleaner water that was a five-hour journey.'

EARLY RELEASE AS A DILEMMA

Let's return to the issue about prisons that we considered earlier. We can frame what appears to be a dilemma in the following way.

If we seek to reduce the prison population by having an early release programme, then we will reduce the (deterrent) effectiveness of the criminal justice system. Alternatively, if we don't have an early release programme, then (through prison overcrowding) we will reduce the (rehabilitative) effectiveness of the criminal justice system. So, whatever we choose to do, we will reduce the effectiveness of the criminal justice system.

We can show this dilemma argument as follows.

If p, then q. If not-p, then q. So, in either case, q.

Here's a different dilemma argument.

If we seek to reduce the prison population by having an early release programme, then we will reduce the effectiveness of the criminal justice system. If we don't spend much more money on the prison service, then we will reduce the effectiveness of the criminal justice system. We're faced with doing one of these things, so we must reduce the effectiveness of the criminal justice system.

This dilemma argument is clearly different from the first. (It's called a 'constructive dilemma'.) Its structure can be shown as follows.

If p, then r. If q, then r. Either p or q have to be done, so r must happen.

ESCAPING FROM DILEMMAS

Dilemmas appear to be pretty troublesome. In this connection, you might well have heard the expression 'being caught on the horns of a dilemma'. This captures the problem well. The two horns of a dilemma are the two conditional premises (reasons) in the form of if...then. A two-horned creature will catch you with one horn if you manage to escape the other. But things aren't necessarily as difficult as that. Dilemmas might be more apparent than real. There might be all sorts of ways to avoid one of the (conditional) horns.

ESCAPING BETWEEN THE HORNS OF A DILEMMA

We could, for example, escape between the horns of the dilemma. We would do this by not accepting that we have no more than p or q. Thus in the second dilemma-argument, we could question whether our choices are exhausted by having an early release scheme or spending more money on the prison service. It could be, for example, that we could make better use of existing spending (by more efficient use of staff and buildings). As a result we have s, which could give us a desired consequence t (we can increase the effectiveness of the criminal justice system). In which case, at one leap, we've escaped the horns of the dilemma (or what was only an apparent dilemma).

TAKING A DILEMMA BY THE HORNS

We could also take a dilemma 'by the horns' such that we simply deny one of the conditional premises. For example, we could simply deny the first conditional in the first argument (that if we seek to reduce the prison population by having an early release programme, then we will reduce the effectiveness of the criminal justice system). We might want to counter-argue that an early release programme improves the criminal justice system by having lower rates of people committing further offences (through a community support programme).

APPARENT DILEMMAS

With both techniques of escaping the horns and taking by the horns, we escape the restrictions implicit in a dilemma. So, in the normal course of events, are we likely to find many dilemmas? We can write them all day long but will we find real examples of true dilemmas that we can reduce to the structure of p and q (and r)? Look at the next one.

> Many countries that have capital punishment see the only choice for very serious offences, such as murder, as being between execution and full life in prison. This is certainly the case in the US. Each of these punishments provokes very serious moral arguments, so any countries that operate them must respond to the moral problems that result.

Has a dilemma been identified?

The answer is, of course, that it depends from which position you see it. For countries such as the US that operate both execution and life without parole for murderers, there is presumably no dilemma. They are likely to accept that there are serious moral arguments with either sentence but that, in each case, the moral arguments justify the sentence. Others who stand outside the system, so to speak, might well stress that the moral arguments are such that neither course of action is normally acceptable (or that one is less unacceptable than the other). But there is no dilemma identified.

CONSEQUENCES OF POLAR OPPOSITES

Dilemmas in which the consequences of two different courses of action are equivalent in their unacceptability are very rare. If the two different courses of action are not balanced then it is likely to make the dilemma uncomfortable but not unresolvable.

Let's look at a policy decision taken by many countries in the world: the decision to forbid smoking in public places. Some countries have not adopted this (for example, Japan and Hungary); some countries have a variable ban (the US is a good example, with variation between states), but many countries have not only banned smoking in public places but are planning to extend the range of the ban.

Once we start to look for possible consequences of the two polar positions ('allow smoking in public places' and its negative), we can see that it's very difficult to nail down what they are. Figure 4.1 shows some of the consequences of one of these positions: allowing smoking in public places.

You can see that some of the consequences take us into areas that are difficult to pin down. For example, how can we put a cost on the enlargement of smokers' freedom (and of its opposite for non-smokers)? But, even more quantifiable outcomes such as health costs are very difficult to pin down. One of the problems is that because the smoker is not likely to live as long as the non-smoker, the health costs of the non-smoking group could in the longer term be higher than those of the smoking group (a point emphasised by the latter group having paid taxes on their tobacco products).

This problem of equivalence of consequences is of considerable significance in approaching decision making in general, as well as dilemmas in particular. In this example, there are so many variables to consider that it is difficult to frame a dilemma that fits with any attempt to reduce it to a formal structure.

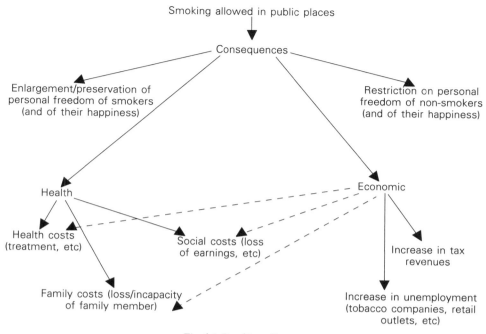

Fig 4.1 Smoking diagram.

When we're dealing with cost-benefit analyses of subjects such as health, we can attempt to look at the cost implications but we need to see these in a far-reaching way. These costs need to include the implications not only for diseases such as cancer, cardio-vascular conditions and respiratory disorders, but also issues such as employment and the wider economy.[8] Social and economic factors show considerable interdependence, making the analysis (indeed the identification) of consequences a very, very difficult area.

And, if we thought the analysis of social and economic consequences was difficult, there are others which are much more difficult to pin down. These are moral consequences that we came across earlier (in the apparent dilemma over capital punishment and life without parole). We'll turn our attention in this direction in the next chapter.

But before we move on, here's an interesting example of an identified consequence being used as the justification for a policy. Singapore is well known as a country that is intolerant of litter. In order to encourage people not to litter (discourage people from littering), fines for first offences for dropping small items such as cigarette butts and sweet wrappers were increased by 50% in 2010. The Minister for the Environment, Yaacob Ibrahin, has stressed the need to 'task people to begin to think of the consequences of their actions'. To emphasise this point he provided an example of someone who throws a cigarette pack wrapper out of a car. 'He may think it's a small (piece of) plastic, but that plastic will fly, go into a drain, accumulate with other litter; it'll clog up our drains – then you get dengue fever.'[9]

NOTES

1. Routledge, 2009. p. 38.
2. F. Fernández-Armesto, *Truth*. Black Swan Books, 1998. p.142.
3. Sir D. King, 'Bovine Tuberculosis in Cattle and Badgers', 2007, www.bis.gov.uk/assets/biscore/corporate/migratedD/ec_group/44-07-S_I_on
4. Source of statistics: *Pocket World in Figures*. Profile Books, 2010. p. 100.
5. 'A game of cat and mouse', *Economist*, 5 June 2010, p. 92.
6. J. Burningham, *Would you rather?* Red Fox, 1994.
7. For a very good example of this, see S. Cassidy, *Audacity to Believe*. Collins, 1977. Especially pp. 172–198.
8. See for example, A. Maryon-Davis, 'Legislating for health-related gain: striking a balance', *Canadian Medical Association Journal*, 2010, 182, pp. 747–48.
9. O. Dai Lin 'Littering: a fine mess', TODAYonline, 7 June 2010, www.todayonline. com/hotnews/EDC100607-0000068/Littering-A-fine-mess

5

ETHICAL ASPECTS OF DECISION MAKING

You will remember that, in the report on TB in badgers and cattle, Sir David King recommended that badgers should be 'removed'. The fact that it was only with the first use of this word that the actual meaning of 'removal' as 'killing' was clarified is probably very significant. If that's what it meant, why didn't Sir David simply use it throughout? Removal could mean 'move from one place to another' as in companies that move house-contents for you. A 'removal firm' does not have the meaning of a company that kills. So why, when in the end Sir David was recommending that hundreds (or thousands) of badgers should be killed, did he use what amounts to a euphemism? Presumably because the word 'removal' sounds less harsh, cruel, unpleasant. This recognition that killing involves a judgemental aspect leads Sir David to stress that 'any removal of badgers must be done humanely and within conservation considerations'. This is certainly very striking. If killing of badgers is being recommended, what is the significance of it being done 'humanely'?

Questions like this take us into the area of ethics. Sir David King might well want many hundreds of dead badgers but he finds himself unable to shake off an ethical concern about the process. Ethics is concerned with how we should live our lives. Should we be generous in giving to charities? Should we tell the truth? Should we keep our promises? By extension, then, it is also concerned with how societies should deal with how people should behave. Should abortion be allowed? Should we experiment on animals? Should we go to war? Should we tolerate behaviour and beliefs of which we disapprove? (And, in each case, why / why not?)

NON-ETHICAL DECISION MAKING

Much decision making can avoid ethical considerations altogether, by focusing exclusively on other aspects of the decision to be made. Even if ethical issues arise, they don't have to be acknowledged or allowed to make any difference to the process or outcome. For example, though the question 'Should we have capital punishment?' has a large ethical component, it could also be seen in purely economic terms. Thus it has been argued (by some US websites) that keeping criminals in prison for life is too expensive, so we can justify executing them on economic grounds.

Similarly, the question, 'Should we experiment on animals for medical purposes?' involves a very large ethical dimension but, again, it could be answered in the affirmative by looking at it in other ways. For example, the UK government used strong legal powers to protect the animal-testing company Huntingdon Life Sciences and to encourage it back to the UK after it moved to the US because of a campaign against it. The justification was centrally economic: the government used the argument that if testing on animals couldn't be done in the UK, it would be done elsewhere.

ETHICAL THEORIES

The title of this chapter suggests that we are going to look at the possible significance of some well-used ethical theories for decision making. For those who want much more detail, there are plenty of books available which will provide it.[1] But, if we are going to do the job of applying ethical theories properly, we do need to be sufficiently clear as to their content.

What do we expect from an ethical theory? At the very least, it should offer some answer to an ethical problem that we have (even if it's an answer that we don't like). If the ethical theory does not offer a solution to our problem, it is of limited value. ('Limited' rather than 'no', because it could still offer some insights, even though it doesn't go all the way to solving the problem.)

We will consider three major ethical theories. We will outline the important content of the theories and apply them to real or hypothetical situations on the way. The ethical theories are:

- Utilitarianism
- Deontological Ethics
- Libertarianism

UTILITARIANISM

You will have come across the word 'utility' before. It means 'usefulness'. The term 'utility room' shows this well, in that it refers to a room where useful appliances are kept (washing machine, dishwasher, tumble dryer, etc.). This meaning of 'usefulness' is significant. Those who look at ethics in terms of 'utility' are looking at what comes out of their ethical theory. They are interested in results (like we're interested in dry clothes coming out of a tumble dryer).

In light of this, it is understandable why Utilitarianism is sometimes called a 'consequentialist' theory. This is because it is centrally concerned with the consequences of actions. What comes out of the process of applying a utilitarian position to a problem?

Ethical questions can be very small. For example, should I tip a waiter in a restaurant? The utilitarian would be interested in that question in terms of what consequences it had. We'll return to this example later. Big questions would include those concerned with a subject we've already spent some time thinking about: Should foreign aid be given to developing countries? The utilitarian would again be interested in the consequences of giving or not giving such aid. We'll come back to this one later too.

What is it about the consequences that the utilitarian is interested in?

KILLING AND CONSEQUENCES

We'll start with a big issue. Let's consider the example of someone killing somebody else. What consequences of this action is the utilitarian interested in? In one form of the theory, they are interested in how such an action affects people's welfare. (We'll look in more detail below at what we mean by this.) In other words, we need to know more about the circumstances of the action in order to judge whether it was a good or bad one. Questions like 'Who was killed?' and 'Why were they killed?' become relevant.

You can see that a general position of 'all killing is wrong' is not one which fits with looking at the consequences of actions. A utilitarian can distinguish between actions in which somebody is killed as sometimes justifiable and sometimes not. To see how this might work, consider these different situations.

- Rudolf Höss, the first Commandant of Auschwitz, was hanged in 1947 as a punishment for his involvement in mass murder.

- Freddy Bywaters was hanged in London in January 1923 for the murder of his lover's husband.

In each of these cases, a legal process was used which led to the killing of someone. Is each of them to be seen in the same way? Were they each right (or wrong)? The utilitarian would need to look at the consequences of each.

If we are looking at the consequences of each of these cases in terms of the effect on 'welfare', how might this work? Perhaps the execution of Höss could be justified in terms of increasing the welfare of all those who suffered under him (but survived) and all those who had relatives who died as a result of his actions (directly or indirectly). We could also bring into the calculation all those who saw Nazism as so abhorrent that the death of such a prominent member of that movement was something that increased their welfare. Of course, we would have to set the welfare of the family and friends of Höss against all this, as well as the welfare of those who supported the Nazi cause. As a result, a calculation could be made to see if welfare had been increased by the execution of Höss. (I would think it was, but you might have done the calculation differently.)

The story of Freddy Bywaters is a tragic love story.[2] He killed only one man (unlike Höss), the husband of his lover. Freddy had a mother, two sisters and a brother. His victim had a brother and two sisters. Neither man had children. Freddy's lover (the victim's wife) was hanged at the same time as him, having been convicted (almost certainly wrongly) of conspiracy to murder. So can the execution of this 20-year-old man be justified in terms of welfare or not? This is much more difficult than the case of Höss.

Though the decision making we're normally concerned with has nothing to do with a choice about whether someone should be deliberately killed, these two examples illustrate a problem very well. Here we have the same action (judicial hanging) in response to *hugely* different crimes. Höss was responsible for killing on a massive scale. Bywaters perhaps didn't even *intend* to kill one person (it is disputed whether he planned to kill his victim). Is the same action therefore utterly out of sync with the justification of that action?

HAPPINESS, WELL-BEING, PLEASURE AND OTHER GOOD THINGS

After considering these examples, it is time to take stock of where we are. The first big name associated with Utilitarianism is Jeremy Bentham (1748–1832). For him, there was something straightforward about what the utilitarian is looking for when we talk about 'welfare'. This is a quality of well-being that people feel. Think about how you feel at the moment. Do you feel more or less happy than you did ten minutes ago? What is the source of your level of happiness? If it is relatively high, would you want it further maximised? If it is relatively low, would you want this low level further minimised?

The classic Utilitarian position as developed by Bentham looks at actions and judges them against a measure of happiness. You will remember the question of whether or not I should tip a waiter in a restaurant. From a utilitarian position, I need to consider the consequences. It's not just a question of looking backwards over the quality of the service that's been provided. It's also very much a question of looking forwards at the consequences of tipping or not tipping.

SOME PROBLEMS OF LOOKING AT AND FOR CONSEQUENCES

This very simple example illustrates well the problems of looking at consequences of decisions. For what are they? In the previous chapter, we raised the problem of identifying consequences of decisions. Where should we draw the line? This was a significant problem with a big decision like banning smoking in public places, with a cost–benefit analysis having to consider a wide range of costs and benefits.

Though he has often been criticised for what he said, the former US Defence Secretary Donald Rumsfeld's famous reference to 'unknown unknowns' in 2002 is a very good description of the problem.

> 'Reports that say that something hasn't happened are always interesting to me, because as we know, there are known knowns; there are things we know we know. We also know there are known unknowns; that is to say we know there are some things we do not know. But there are also unknown unknowns – the ones we don't know we don't know.'

So what *known knowns* follow my decision to give, say, a 10% tip to my waiter? One is that I'm worse off financially by whatever the 10% represents. Another is that my waiter is equivalently better off. (Although, of course, it's not as simple as that: the equivalence of the transaction depends centrally on our respective income levels.) In that I've given the tip, I might say that a known known is what gratification I have in giving the tip. Beyond these, I'm less certain. We're heading towards the next category.

This is *known unknowns*. I, as the tipper, can identify many of these. Examples would be the following.

- What gratification the waiter has in receiving the tip. Is it high ('How generous – that'll help a lot')? Is it low ('Is that all – that's not going to make much difference')?

- What the waiter will spend the money on. This is a known unknown with limitless possibilities. Perhaps the waiter will use it to buy food for his or her hungry family (with higher welfare in consequence). Perhaps it will be used to buy cigarettes and so my tip will contribute to the waiter's future smoking-related illness (with consequences way beyond the immediate ones – employment, welfare of family and so on). Perhaps it will be given to a beggar that they see on their way home from work (with a consequent increase in welfare or its opposite: diswelfare – for the beggar who uses it to buy cheap alcohol, and so sleeps happily that night or falls in a drunken haze beneath a passing lorry). Perhaps it will be used to buy a lottery ticket and they win the jackpot and their life (and with it, countless others) is utterly transformed (to some extent like in Roald Dahl's *Charlie and the Chocolate Factory*). Perhaps, perhaps, perhaps...

- What I might have otherwise spent the money on (with consequences as above).

- What effect my giving a tip will have on the wage level paid to staff in the restaurant. This is an often-given consequence. Employers know that customers will give tips, so they pay their staff correspondingly less than is desirable. This then becomes an issue for the restaurant (and similar) trade in general.

- What effect my giving a tip will have on employment in this restaurant (and others). Perhaps, because of the point above, the owner of this restaurant will employ more people, so increasing welfare (in the employed, their families, their neighbourhood shops and services, and so on).

So what about the third category: *unknown unknowns*?

It would seem as if the logic of the language used is such that we can't say anything here. By definition, we can't identify these. But perhaps we can try to glimpse something through the mist.

What we can say is that we don't where the consequences will stop (or where we should stop looking for them) or whether there are consequences that we simply haven't thought of. So, for example, our now tipped waiter heads away from his or her shift at the restaurant, spends the tip on a copy of this book, gets excited by the value of thinking clearly, decides to study law, becomes a barrister, successfully defends various innocent people (with consequent surges in welfare), goes into politics, becomes Prime Minister, increases public expenditure (with consequent large surges in welfare)...

This example illustrates nicely a significant problem of using consequences as the ethical basis of decision making. And, having seen the complexity of the task with something as relatively small as giving (or not giving) tips, our other example of foreign aid is something that is obviously fearsomely difficult to pin down. Perhaps a possible solution is to narrow down the focus as we did with our tipping example. Thus instead of asking the question, 'Can we justify giving foreign aid?', we find a very specific example such as a small community in a developing country and consider possible consequences of giving x amount of aid to it (specified in terms of what the aid is for, how it's given, and how its use is to be monitored). Then we could do a cost–benefit analysis of this small example from which we can possibly generalise to further (similar) situations. In turn, we could specify the timeframe to look for measurable short-term consequences (from which we might be able to predict medium-term consequences, based on a set of given assumptions).

The Benthamite principle of justifying actions in terms of their effect on happiness is well known as applying the rule of looking to maximise 'the greatest happiness of the greatest number'. This seems to be a simple yardstick to understand, but as we have seen in our consideration of consequences, it is not necessarily a simple yardstick to apply. It has a familiar appeal to public opinion about it, but using public opinion isn't necessarily a very good guide to the value of a proposed decision.

So far, then, we have been looking for a principle that we can use in deciding what course of action can be justified better than another one. The principle of utility involves calculating the effect on people's welfare. We have described this as well-being or happiness. More specifically, we should see it as 'felt' well-being or happiness. In other words, it's not just me reporting that you are happier, it's that you actually feel happier.

J.S. MILL: DIFFERENT LEVELS OF HAPPINESS

One of the most impressive British philosophers was John Stuart Mill (1806–73). He thought that this way of looking at happiness by calculating the justification of actions is too simple. It ignores the way in which different people experience happiness in different ways. Thus Mill argued that there are different levels of happiness. He is often quoted as saying that it is better to be a dissatisfied Socrates than a satisfied fool. Thus there are higher and lower pleasures. Listening to Mozart might be seen as a higher pleasure; watching a football match might be seen as a lower one. Flying Singapore Airlines might be experienced as a higher pleasure than flying Ryanair.

We won't spend much time on this point, but we'll note its significance. This is that to work out the consequences of an action, policy or decision might well be even more complicated than we'd already considered. There is, for example, the additional problem of how keenly a person feels about something. In this way, listening to Mozart might well give someone pleasure, but the joy of watching a football match could be felt much more keenly. Someone flying Ryanair might reflect on how much money they've saved and what they could do with that money. This point could also take us back to the problem of justifying capital punishment in particular cases. It could be that the knowledge that Höss had been executed caused a sense of very high well-being by those who'd suffered at his hands. As a result, should this experience be counted as more important than how others experienced it?

MAXIMISING PREFERENCES

A further way of considering the utilitarian position is to look not at welfare, well-being, happiness or pleasure, but to look at preferences. A decision can be justified if it satisfies people's preferences. If it satisfies more people's preferences than a different decision, then we're okay. This gets round the higher/lower pleasures problem. We might have difficulties accepting some people's preferences, but at least we avoid having to make judgements about them. The psychologists would, of course, fret about what are real preferences and an economist might want to remind us that when we think we're making rational choices based on our preferences, then we are very likely not to be.[3]

You will probably already have thought that, at a very important level, all this talk of maximising preferences (or whatever) fits with the way in which much decision making is done. International organisations such as the United Nations use something of a democratic voting system; small, local organisations do the same. To say that we shouldn't make decisions (political, social, economic, organisational, group and even individual decisions) according to people's preferences in at least some contexts would be seen as requiring a justification. We would expect an explanation of why we shouldn't. (Clearly in much technical decision making, the decision to be taken will not be based on preferences as such but on the nature of the evidence.)

APPLYING UTILITARIANISM TO AN EXAMPLE: VIOLENT COMPUTER GAMES

We'll try to apply what we've considered so far to a frequently discussed issue.

What should we do about violent computer games?

We'll produce a possible continuum of choice and see how a utilitarian perspective might help us to make decisions on this question.

- Encourage people to play violent computer games in the hope of reducing the chances of their being violent themselves. (A)
- Do nothing about the problem of violent computer games. (B)
- Commission further research in order to demonstrate any effects of violent computer games. (C)
- Encourage parents to exercise control over their children by monitoring what games they play. (D)
- Restrict the sales of the most violent computer games only to those aged 18 or over. (E)
- Restrict the sales of all computer games in which violence is portrayed only to those aged 18 or over. (F)
- Ban all computer games for which there is any evidence linking them with violent behaviour. (G)
- Ban all computer games in which the violence is more than 'mild'. (H)
- Ban all computer games in which there is any violence. (I)

How might a utilitarian perspective help us to decide which of these positions to go for? There would be lots of things that must be taken into account. For example, we can't ignore the fact that behaving violently might produce lots of happiness for some people, be their preference, and so on. But we'll look at our options in as simple a way as possible.

There could be a problem with (G), (H) and (I) in relation to the preferences (happiness, pleasure, well-being) of those who play these games. Alternatively, we could look at the preferences (etc.) of those who want these games banned. If there was evidence showing that these games did increase the likelihood that players used violence, then we would also have to look at the well-being (etc.) of those who would be the victims. But what about the welfare of games producers, distributors, sellers, reviewers, etc.?

(E) and (F) restrict the preferences (etc.) of those under 18. We might not think this is a problem. After all, we don't normally give the vote to those under 18. But if lots of young people found their welfare much reduced by these decisions, then we have to be able to answer the charge that welfare has been reduced.

(A) has a welfare-maximising look about it. We could justify this proposal in terms of the consequences. If playing the games made people less violent, then welfare is increased on a big scale (unless you are a police or prison officer, in that you might be made redundant). There is, of course, the problem that we might have got it wrong. Encouraging people to play the games could make them more violent.

(B) can be supported by the utilitarian if doing nothing maximises welfare. This would work if any adverse effects of people playing violent computer games were more than compensated for by the overall level of welfare resulting from doing nothing. For example, we would need to add in the welfare of players (and that of the games producers, etc.), and the fact that presumably most people aren't too worried about the whole issue.

(C) looks to a future situation in which we can maximise welfare only by knowing more about the problem. It can be defended in a utilitarian way by arguing that, once we have established whether or not there are any effects (good or bad), then we can act to maximise welfare. There's also, of course, the increased welfare of the researchers who are employed.

(D) works to maximise welfare by coming up with a solution which could have beneficial effects on overall welfare. The welfare of the controlled children might well be reduced but, if these games have negative effects, then this reduction in welfare could be defended.

PROBLEMS WITH USING UTILITARIANISM IN DECISION MAKING

We have seen, then, that a utilitarian position can illuminate decision making. But we have identified some problems on the way, so we can now turn our attention to look more explicitly at problems with this position.

We're going to look at how workable this ethical theory is. In that we're looking at an ethical theory earning its keep in terms of how much it helps us make decisions, this is very important. Some questions will throw light on what we need to consider.

- How can we rate different types of pleasure?
- How do we rate different levels of experiencing pleasure?
- How can we establish what people's preferences are?
- What if someone's (or some group's) preferences change?
- Whose preferences should we take into account?
- Should preferences be changed?
- How do we know if or when we have maximised welfare?

HOW CAN WE RATE DIFFERENT TYPES OF PLEASURE? HOW DO WE RATE DIFFERENT LEVELS OF EXPERIENCING PLEASURE?

The first and second questions both share the same problem of how we do the necessary calculation of expected pleasure, etc. Even if we have to make very small-scale choices, the calculation of expected welfare is not necessarily easy. Let us suppose someone is faced with a choice between two holiday destinations. If they'd like to go to either of them, how do they do the happiness calculation? They would presumably look at things like facilities, weather, cost and journey times. But, even then, there are problems giving exact figures for the calculation. (How do they rate two rather than two and a half hours on the plane?) What about all the less predictable factors? What about seeing poverty or cruelty to animals at their destination? How do they add those in? Your response could well be that most people are not doing calculations in as detailed a way as this. This is an important point, and raises a number of issues.

- If people don't maximise their own preferences, then why should systems (political, economic, etc.) seek to do this for them?

- If people do very limited calculations of their own preferences, then it is important to know what is included in these calculations. Is cost the dominant criterion? Is time? Is convenience (however we describe that)?

- What are the limits of the information that people want to have in order to make different types of calculations?

If individuals are prepared to accept an overall judgement, rather than, say, being able to produce a result which can be expressed in exact terms (a welfare calculation of, say, $+14$ contrasted with one of -6), then perhaps we shouldn't fret too much about the problems of doing detailed calculations of welfare in decision making. And, in a similar way, we can't expect organisations (including governments) to do the happiness calculation in a very, very detailed form. Perhaps all that we can expect is that they are in the right preference-based direction.

HOW CAN WE ESTABLISH WHAT PEOPLE'S PREFERENCES ARE?

Trying to find out what people's preferences are is a very big and complex area. It involves looking at important and complex areas such as honesty, needs/wants and maturity.

There's also the area of behavioural irrationality referred to above in relation to economic decision making. If someone or some organisation's preferences are at important levels irrational, then how should we respond? Should we give irrational preferences the same status as those that are seen as rational? An example here is that of official attitudes to those who choose to end their lives when they have a terminal illness. The campaign in the UK by Debbie Purdy, suffering from multiple sclerosis, to ensure that her husband wouldn't be charged with a criminal offence if he helped her to commit suicide is a good example of this. Wanting to die prematurely, so to speak, when one is suffering from a terminal (and increasingly distressing) condition is seen by many as an unacceptable preference. But is it?

There are, however, many instances in which we wouldn't have to ask for people's preferences. There are some preferences that, by and large, we can take for granted. For example, should we have a policy that forbids cars from overtaking? I don't even have to go and ask people to know where their preferences lie. We can answer questions like this on the basis of our own judgement, which we can safely generalise to most (all?) others. To give another example, in various places there are barriers which are topped by severely spiked metal constructions. The intention of these sharply spiked barriers is obviously to deter us from climbing over them. Those who installed them didn't have to make much of a judgement as to how unappealing they would be to our welfare. They were correct in assessing them as something that most of us would rather not end up climbing over.

There is not the scope here to consider methodological issues of survey design and questionnaire construction, but both of these would be very relevant to this question.

WHAT IF SOMEONE'S (OR SOME GROUP'S) PREFERENCES CHANGE?

If we are describing a position/decision/recommendation as justified by the preferences of those seen as relevant to the decision-making process, then this question raises an important point. What is justified at point x might be no longer justified at point y, if preferences change. In this way, a decision can be both right and wrong. The example of capital punishment is a good example. Whereas it used to be supported by the majority of people in the UK, it no longer is. So, based on preferences as the key to ethical decisions, executing people in the UK used to be ethical; now it isn't. This will be very difficult for those who see ethical positions as having an absolute quality, such that things are either right or they're not.

Why preferences change is an important area for consideration. It could well be that more information becomes available. The issue of vaccination against MMR (measles, mumps and rubella) is an instructive one. The publication of research, which appeared to show a causal link between the MMR vaccine and autism in the medical journal *The Lancet* in 1998, led to a significant decline in the number of parents in the UK having their children vaccinated. This in turn led, not surprisingly, to an increase in the number of children getting these diseases. However, it was subsequently shown that the research was deeply flawed and those who conducted it, notably Andrew Wakefield, have since been shown to have been 'dishonest' in their research. Vaccination rates have subsequently increased. The decline and then the increase in the vaccination rate are good examples of preferences changing along with changes in information.

WHOSE PREFERENCES SHOULD WE TAKE INTO ACCOUNT?

The fifth question is a very important one. Should everyone's preferences be taken into account? Anyway, what do we mean by 'everyone'? Does it include children? Does it include animals? Does it include future generations of people? (You will remember the big problems with this from Chapter 2.)

For example, the question 'Should we use experiments on animals to research cystic fibrosis?' is one where we centrally need to consider whose preferences are to be taken into account. Is it just those families which have a child with the condition (or whose adults carry the gene responsible for the condition)? What about those who are opposed to animal experimentation? What about research staff who work in this area? And, of course, what about the welfare/well-being/happiness/preferences of the animals that will be used?

In medium to large organisations (such as commercial companies and government departments), we very much have the issue of whose preferences are important. Those who manage companies might well argue that there is a ranking in importance of preferences, such that their preferences are of greater significance than those being managed. As a result, the quality of the decisions will be judged not by overall preferences but by those who manage. Thus the justification of employing various directors of departments (finance, human resources, IT, marketing and so on) at very high salaries when secretarial staff are given minimal pay increases (if any at all) is based not on overall preferences but on those from a narrow range. Whether or not welfare is maximised is then a very difficult question to answer. This is, of course, a very big area for analysis.

In big organisations, there might well be people who, through deference or laziness (or whatever), will choose (express a preference) not to express their position. This contradictory position can be put as simply as, 'I'm not paid to think'. Thus changes in organisational functioning to allow people at all levels to show initiative, find things out and such like might be seen as a problem for the welfare for some. But it could be seen as an increase in welfare for others. This problem of conflicting preferences is a very difficult one to solve, and takes us to the next problem.

SHOULD PREFERENCES BE CHANGED?

'Sometimes, the key to success lies in tempering aspirations.'[4] This point comes from an article in June 2010 about the Singapore government's need to shift their citizens' preferences away from wanting a car to using public transport. By reducing people's ability to acquire cars through reductions in what are called 'Certificates of Entitlement', and by stressing the benefits of living in a city with unpolluted air, the Transport Minister seeks to 'temper aspirations' or, as we might put it in more utilitarian terms, 'shift preferences'. Clearly, if preferences can be changed, then the pursuit of welfare is towards a different outcome.

There are lots of issues here. Does a decision maker simply factor preferences into the process or are various considerations taken into account, such as how informed the preferences are? This would be relevant, for example, when people's preferences are not based on a full appreciation of all the relevant information. This brings in questions of what would be people's real preferences if they knew more (or, of course, if they were more critical in their thinking).

HOW DO WE KNOW IF OR WHEN WE HAVE MAXIMISED WELFARE?

This question very much links to the previous one. If maximising welfare is concerned with achieving a final outcome, then the nature of this final outcome can be changed by 'tempering aspirations'.

But there is a central problem, anyway, with this question. It's not as if, having done the happiness calculation, we hear a bell ring showing we've maximised it. We never really know when we've done it, especially when we're looking at decision making on a big scale. But, apart from the difficulties identified when looking at the earlier questions in this section, there's a separate but very important point relevant to this question. Quite simply, we don't know what would have happened if we hadn't implemented this decision.

For example, let's say we ban all computer games in which there is any violence (option I). In calculating the effects of this, we can't know what doing nothing (option B) would have done in relation to people's preferences. We can't rerun the tape to see. In this way, maximising welfare becomes difficult to judge.

DOES UTILITARIANISM HELP US TO KNOW HOW TO DISTRIBUTE SCARCE RESOURCES?

Many political decisions involve the question of how we should distribute welfare amongst the population. For example, there have been recent campaigns in the UK concerned with demands that all people who need them should receive specific drugs through the National Health Service (NHS). This is a real issue and it is not necessarily easily resolved. Just to say 'give all of them the drugs' is likely to ignore the complexities of the problem. In one recent case, protests that people with brain tumours should all receive a specific course of drug treatment was countered by a NHS decision maker with the point that, if that were to happen, then there would be a knock-on effect elsewhere to cover the cost (say, fewer hip replacements or scanning machines). Utilitarianism is very relevant to trade-offs such as this.

Let's look at this with an imaginary scenario.

A country's population can be broken down into five groups, based on their existing levels of welfare.

- 10% of the population have very low levels of welfare (through poverty, for example).
- 15% of the population have low levels of welfare.
- 50% of the population have moderate levels of welfare.

- 15% of the population have high levels of welfare.
- 10% of the population have very high levels of welfare (through considerable affluence, for example).

There are 1,000,000 people in the country so they are therefore distributed as follows.

1. 100,000 people with very low levels of welfare.
2. 150,000 people with low levels of welfare.
3. 500,000 people with moderate levels of welfare.
4. 150,000 people with high levels of welfare.
5. 100,000 people with very high levels of welfare.

A new drug is available that could cure a life-threatening disease. But the health service can't afford to give this drug to all who need it. In this country, there are 200 people with the life-threatening disease, distributed evenly amongst the welfare groups (the disease is no respecter of felt welfare). The health service has enough funding to give the drug to only 100 people. Who should these be?

If it gave the drug to 20 from each category, then what happens? It means that the level of welfare has stayed the same.

Perhaps the policy could be adopted of giving the drug to the 40 people in the very low welfare group and the 40 in the low welfare group, with the remaining 20 coming from the moderate welfare group. This could be a policy of 'positive discrimination', concentrating resources where there is least welfare. But what would be the outcome of this policy? Quite simply, the level of overall welfare would decline. We would lose people from the high and very high welfare groups, with insufficient compensatory gain.

What then happens if we give the drug to the 40 in the high welfare group and to the 40 in the very high welfare group, with the remaining 20 who get it in the group from those with moderate welfare? Given that people in the low and very low welfare groups now die, our overall level of welfare has increased. As simple as that. Nice.

Of course, for a full calculation of the consequences for welfare, we would need to look at the welfare of all those who would be affected by our decisions. For example, person P from the very high welfare group might have no family and friends and thus their death would be unmourned. Q, however, from the very low welfare group might be greatly mourned by his seven children. (Think of Scrooge and Bob Cratchit in Charles Dickens' *Christmas Carol*.)

At one level, then, the utilitarian position allows us to see that an uncritical nod in the direction of equality might not be an ethically defensible thing to do. In terms of decision making, the position provides at the very least a practical framework for choosing between different options.

The previous discussion has hinted at how utilitarianism can provide rules for how we ought to act. It is perhaps not surprising, therefore, that there is a version of the theory called 'rule utilitarianism'. A rule utilitarian position is one which says that we should act in ways that, if everybody were to act in that way, welfare would be maximised. The example we considered at the end of the previous chapter – the possible consequence of throwing away a cigarette packet wrapper – fits well here. If everybody followed the rule of disposing of their litter with more attention to the consequences of not doing so, overall welfare would increase. Therefore each of us should dispose of our litter with a concern for the consequences of not doing so. The rule avoids us having to get caught up with individual exceptions, such as those who get pleasure from releasing their cigarette packet wrapper out of their car window.

DOESN'T UTILITARIANISM MERELY ENCOURAGE SELFISHNESS?

In that we have been looking at criteria such as pleasure, happiness and preferences, it might be thought that utilitarianism is just a licence to maximise our own pleasures without a thought for anyone else.

There is a companion ethical theory called 'egoism'. ('Ego' is the Latin for 'I'.) This theory is concerned with the need for each person to act in ways that maximise their welfare. This does not mean that a person living their life according to this theory will act in ways that do not consider others. For example, you might want to act in ways that take other people's feelings or interest into account. You might want to devote yourself to the care of others.

We won't concern ourselves too much with egoism here because we are looking at how ethical theories can help us with decision making on a scale beyond the individual. It can be noted, however, that egoism avoids some of the problems with utilitarianism. The obvious one is that we don't have to try to calculate preferences across the board: just your own is enough. (Although, even here, we have the psychological problem of identifying your own real preferences.)

CONSEQUENCES AND TRADE-OFFS

Utilitarianism provides a familiar way of dealing with choices and it seems to fit well with how many choices are dealt with. Here's another example from Singapore.

In May 2010 the Minister for Law, K. Shanmugam, defended the use of the death penalty for drug traffickers on the basis that 'there are always trade-offs'. He was responding to questions about a 22 year old who had been given a stay of execution following his conviction for transporting 47g of heroin into Singapore from Malaysia. With regard to the issue of 'trade-offs', he argued that the law against trafficking was important because 'the danger to a large number of others is not obvious'. If the 22 year old wasn't executed, the consequences, he stressed, would be unacceptable. 'You save one life here, but ten other lives will be gone. What would your choice be?' If he isn't executed, then 'drug barons will think that the signal is that young and vulnerable traffickers will be spared and can be used as drug mules. Then you'll get ten more. There'll be an unstoppable stream of such people. . .'[5]

Whatever we look at, the issue of consequences is never far away. But we're going to shift away from them for a while. We're going to move from utility to duty.

DEONTOLOGICAL ETHICS

We have seen that utilitarianism focuses on the consequences of actions: an action is right if it maximises welfare. In this way, the utilitarian is concerned with what follows a decision rather than the decision itself. If we disagree with a particular decision, the utilitarian could say, 'Wait until you see what happens, and then you'll see that the decision was right.'

But we might want to respond that we don't think that the decision was right in the first place. Whatever the consequences, the decision might be one that we find ethically unacceptable. For example, when we look back at our continuum of choice for violent computer games, we might find (A) ethically unacceptable, even if it did lead to people becoming less violent. We might want to say that there is something unacceptable about children playing violent games and that's enough to rule out (A).

This emphasis upon choices being right or wrong in themselves finds us in the system of ethics called 'deontological'. The term 'deontological' comes from two Greek words: *deon* meaning 'one must' and *logos* meaning 'science' (think of words such as biology and psychology). The two components of the word are both important for an understanding of the significance of the term.

KANT'S REASONED ETHICS

The name normally associated with duty ethics is Immanuel Kant (1724–1804). There are many aspects of Kant's account of ethics, and we shall concentrate only on how we can apply a deontological position to decision making. The link between 'duty' and 'science' is, for Kant, a central point. The study of how we should behave and the laws of nature are, for him, linked. In other words, we can study both of these subjects as rational creatures. How we should behave is therefore a question that can be answered, if you like, scientifically. (As, of course, it can be by the utilitarians with their emphasis on preferences and consequences.)

Kant argued that if we look at all life (animal and plant), then every part of an organism has a purpose. In fish, fins are there to help them swim; in dogs, their considerable ability to analyse scents is useful for hunting. Animals, he argued, are controlled by instinct: the bee, for example, does not seek out pollen as a result of reflecting on what to do with its day. Humans, however, are more than instinct, since they have the capacity to reason. Thus, according to Kant, if the pursuit of happiness were enough for us, we wouldn't need reason. Animals can seek to maximise their welfare through instinct. We must do something other than this.

Kant argued that all rational human beings would (have to) agree on what is the general duty which can be applied to all situations. It is, in fact, much stronger than 'can be applied': Kant saw the duty as being an absolute one, such that rational people would have to apply it. It's like saying, 'Should I use this 100 centimetre stick as the one to mark out metres or should I use the 95 centimetre one?' The question has only one answer for a rational person.

ETHICAL DUTIES

So what is this ethical duty which we must accept? Kant argued that we should act only in such a way that we could accept that this way of acting should apply to everyone.

It will be helpful to consider how this might work in practice. Consider why telling the truth is something that we should do. How would it fit with Kant's required ethical duty? If we look at what would happen if everyone lied, then we could not wish this to be required action. If everyone lied, communication would be impossible. So I cannot wish it to be a universal law that everyone lies. It becomes therefore a duty to tell the truth. Though this looks like an example of rule utilitarianism, there is an important difference. We are not justifying telling the truth in terms of welfare, but in terms of the impossibility of a rational person wanting the lack of truth-telling to be the norm. You could try the same exercise with keeping promises.

Kant's account could be seen as having the problem of not allowing exceptions. There is a problem with the absolute duty not to lie in that we can think of situations where telling a lie could be seen as an entirely acceptable thing to do.

HOW DO WE SEE ETHICAL DUTIES?

But has Kant come up with something that fits well with how we see the world? Though there will be some things that might have a value (keeping promises, telling the truth, being considerate to others and so on) relative to the situation in which we find ourselves, are there some actions that we can never accept, regardless of the consequences? What about killing a child? In his book *The Holocaust*, Martin Gilbert[6] describes an event in which German soldiers attacked a hospital and threw babies out of an upper-storey window for their comrades below to catch on their bayonets. Why is it that your reaction to that information is, I expect, the same as mine? Are we both using an absolute moral judgement, such that we can never accept that this is justified? (Although, since presumably it was able to be justified by those doing it at that time, the notion of an absolute moral judgement is a problem.)

Has Kant got things right on the killing of children? Indeed, Kant went further and argued that there is an absolute moral duty not to kill innocent people. (He had no problem with killing animals or justifying the execution of murderers.) Some recent evidence might suggest that there is a problem in how we perceive this moral duty.

In a study,[7] volunteers were given two problems. In the first, a runaway train threatens to kill five people on the track ahead, but their deaths can be prevented by a bystander throwing a lever, thus switching the train to a different track causing only the one person on this track to die. In the second, the bystander can save the five by throwing someone in front of the train, thus killing this person. Though both cases involve killing one person to save five, most thought it correct to do so in the first but not the second case. Brain scans of the volunteers revealed that they used the logical part of the brain to solve the first problem, but the part of the brain that deals with emotions to solve the second.

So Kant is faced here with the problem that we don't always approach moral problems rationally. Our brains appear to be 'hard-wired' to prevent us being as thoroughly Kantian as we might like to be. However, the study also shows that we're not as utilitarian as we might seem to be. In both cases, the principle of utility would point us in the direction of sacrificing one person to save the people in the train.

Various studies have looked at how people would approach decision making in health care. They show an interesting combination of utilitarian and deontological approaches. In one study in Brazil,[8] members of the public were asked to make choices as to who should get treatment between different types of patient. For example, if a 7-year-old child and a 65-year-old man were both victims of a car accident, which of them should get a hospital bed? 72% said that the child should get the bed. The justifications included deontological reasons – 'The child must be protected' – and utilitarian ones – 'The life expectancy and potential of the child is greater'. However, when the two cases were a 25-year-old man and a 65-year-old man, 61% chose the older man. Justifications included the deontological, 'He is older, therefore he is weaker'. However, some of the 36% who chose the younger man reasoned, in a utilitarian way, that 'The younger one has to be attended first because he can do useful work'.

What studies such as this one show is that making decisions can, in practice, involve more than one ethical theory. The way we make choices is not necessarily either utilitarian or deontological, but a combination of the two.

APPLYING THE ETHICS OF DUTY TO DECISION MAKING

But let's see if we can start applying a deontological framework to decision making. We will return to the continuum of choice as to what to do with violent computer games. We're now going to look at where absolute moral duties are going to take us with this problem. Gone is talk of maximising preferences for the different policies. We will need to judge them against the requirement of moral duties, such that we are concerned with the morality of the decision itself.

If we take it that we have an absolute moral duty not to kill innocent people, then we can consider that we have a similar duty to prevent violence against innocent people. It surely can't be right to almost kill an innocent person, but not to kill them. How would this apply to our continuum on violent computer games? If it could be shown that violent computer games did contribute to actual violence, then we are looking at a moral duty to ban them. If the case is yet to be proved, then we must justify decisions on the basis of having a moral duty to reduce the risk of harm to innocent people. Let's have this in front of us while we're doing this exercise.

- Encourage people to play violent computer games in the hope of reducing the chances of them being violent themselves. (A)
- Do nothing about the problem of violent computer games. (B)
- Commission further research in order to demonstrate any effects of violent computer games. (C)
- Encourage parents to exercise control over their children by monitoring what games they play. (D)
- Restrict the sales of the most violent computer games only to those aged 18 or over. (E)
- Restrict the sales of all computer games in which violence is portrayed only to those aged 18 or over. (F)
- Ban all computer games for which there is any evidence linking them with violent behaviour. (G)
- Ban all computer games in which the violence is more than 'mild'. (H)
- Ban all computer games in which there is any violence. (I)

We could take a precautionary position and defend all those from (E) to (I) on the basis that these could fit with our moral duty to prevent harm. But (B) is a problem for our moral duty position if we are concerned with the possibility of harm. Indeed (B) can be justified deontologically only if it could be shown that our moral duty not to harm others is best served by doing nothing. (C) could be defended on the grounds that we should do this in order to be clearer as to how our moral duty to prevent harm fits with the problem. Of course, we could justify doing any of (E) to (I) and also (C) together on the same basis.

This leaves (A) and (D). We could defend (A) but only if we have evidence that it would work to prevent harm. Without such evidence, we appear to be treating our moral duty in rather a weak way. (D) could be supported if it worked. We might need to remind parents of their moral duty to prevent harm for this to work. In consequence, 'encourage' looks too weak. 'Require' would fit better with a moral duty.

DIFFERENT RULES?

Some writers have referred to a set of rules that are absolute; others have seen the need to balance some rules against others. The way in which the rules are interpreted can also vary. For example, W.D. Ross argued that we have a duty to do as much good as possible. Other deontologists have responded by saying that this duty of 'beneficence' means no more than being required to do something for those who are in need. Some have argued that our duties are not as demanding as they appear. If we are not in breach of our duty, they would argue that we can do what we like in our own time. We can, of course, also go beyond duty. Examples would include those who helped Jewish people in Nazi-occupied Europe – not just the famous Oscar Schindler and Raoul Wallenberg, but also uncounted unknown brave people.

DUTIES, ENDS AND MEANS

We have so far stressed that the deontological position requires us to focus on duty as the basis for our decision making. However, things are rather more complicated than that. Kant stressed that the ability to act as an autonomous person was the central thing that we should ensure. In other words, the ability to determine the way in which we lead our life was something that could not be traded off against other things (such as maximising people's preferences). Kant tapped into a very old idea of not treating people as means to ends. To take autonomous people and simply use them as a means to an end (however good this end might be) cannot be justified. The policy of giving someone a severe sentence (for example, life without parole) for their crime on the ground that it would deter others is a big problem here. Deterrent sentences use one person (or persons) as the means of deterring others.

RAWLS

Another name of note in the deontological position is that of John Rawls (1921–2002). His book *A Theory of Justice*[9] was one of the most important books of the second half of the twentieth century. We have not got space to look in detail at his theory, but we can note some things that are useful in decision making.

THE VEIL OF IGNORANCE

He developed the idea of considering what sort of society we would have if we had to choose behind what he called a 'veil of ignorance'. This works by requiring us to make choices on questions like, 'Should we tolerate poverty?' 'Should we discriminate on the grounds of age in relation to jobs?' 'Should we prevent some groups of people from having health care, such as expensive drugs?' But, behind the veil of ignorance, we make the choices without knowing anything about who we would be in our society. For all we know we could be poor, homeless, very sick and so on. We could be male or female, young or old, attractive or unattractive. If we wouldn't be prepared to accept any position in the society that we're agreeing to behind the veil of ignorance, then we can't justify it for others. If I'm not prepared to be homeless, why should I accept that others could be?

This idea of the veil of ignorance has been criticised for being something that is impossible to apply. We can't imagine ourselves in a disembodied form, having no idea of our age, gender, ethnic group and so on. But the idea still has value in focusing us on whether or not we can justify inequalities. It might well be that we could accept being less affluent than others, as long as our position was still tolerable.

THE DIFFERENCE PRINCIPLE

This brings us to another of Rawls' ideas. This is known as the 'difference principle'. By this he means that we can tolerate social and economic differences if they work to the benefit of the least advantaged. A good example could be the considerable wealth held by some people (Lakshmi Mittal, Richard Branson, Alan Sugar and so on). If it could be shown that the wealth of such people benefited not only them, but also the least advantaged people in their society (or, more relevantly, the global economy), then we can tolerate their being so wealthy. An obvious example of such a benefit would be employment. People can get jobs in the Mittal steel companies, with Virgin Atlantic and in one of the hotels owned by Lord Sugar. Try out the difference principle on other examples of inequality.

We are likely to find these two ideas of Rawls – the veil of ignorance and the difference principle – helpful in decision making. Can we justify a particular decision (a choice from the continuum) on the basis that we would be prepared to occupy any of the positions affected by it? Think back to the issue of pay differentials that we discussed earlier. Can we, for example, justify giving pay increases only to the top level of management from the perspective of the lowest paid? (Would we be prepared to be one of the lowest paid in such an organisation?) Can disproportionately rewarding the top level of management be justified on the basis that by doing so the least advantaged are benefited (by, for example, being able to recruit especially good managers)? If a company rewards its partners particularly well (regardless of their competence and how hard they work) because it's been a good financial year but tells the lower paid that they can't receive bonuses because there's not enough to give them, then we have a double problem!

Rawls was critical of the utilitarians because their position would not fit well with either the veil of ignorance or the difference principle. He goes as far as saying that behind the veil of ignorance, we wouldn't pick utilitarianism as a guide to what we should do. He points out that one of the problems with it is that it doesn't distinguish between different desires. For example, someone who wants to discriminate on the grounds of age ('You can't have that job any more because your hair is grey') might be allowed to exercise that preference in utilitarianism, but not with his position.

We'll have a look at how the Rawlsian position would help us in decision making later.

LIBERTARIANISM

Rawls (and Kant) saw the notion of a right as a central feature in their ethics. Rawls argues that we shouldn't be neutral about taking into account people's preferences. If you enjoy seeing other people enjoy much less welfare than you do, then you are not entitled to this enjoyment. Your enjoyment is wrong because it goes against a principle that you would have agreed to behind the veil of ignorance. Thus Rawls is not looking to maximise preferences whatever they are. He is stressing that the idea of a right comes before the idea of preferences.

However, there are rights and there are rights. The libertarian (as the word suggests) is concerned with liberty. Indeed, their concern for liberty is paramount. Just as the utilitarian is concerned with maximising preferences, and the deontologist is concerned with stressing duty, so the libertarian is concerned with preserving freedom. We sometimes see the term used in newspaper accounts referring to people who think that the State has gone too far. (They condemn what they call 'Statism', even though they use the power of the State to achieve what they consider to be the best policies.) For example, some libertarians argue that the State should not get involved with restricting the use of presently illegal drugs or regulating sexual behaviour.

NOZICK

Libertarians focus on the relationship between the individual and the State. In doing this, they start from the position of the rights of the individual. These come first, and the State has to respect them. Though there are many libertarian writers, there is one who is the most significant of recent times. This is Robert Nozick (1938–2002). In some ways, his book *Anarchy, State, and Utopia*[10] was a libertarian response to Rawls. Interestingly, Kant's emphasis on not treating people as means to ends finds a home with Nozick just as it had with Rawls. However, with Nozick, this idea justifies the almost over-riding rights of the individual.

In some ways, Nozick's theory is very simple. Imagine that you're one of the first people to arrive at a previously undiscovered island. Nobody else lives there. You have got acres of uncultivated land available. In order to live, you start cultivating the land, growing a range of fruit and vegetables. You work hour after hour in the hot sun, looking after your plants. The other people who came to this land with you are busy getting on with cultivating their plants in their own parts of the island. Everything is as it should be. Then, one day, another ship arrives at your island. The people come on to your island and, being hungry (and less disposed to work hard), they start to pick your fruit and vegetables. Despite your protests that this produce is yours, they gorge themselves day after day on what you have grown. You'd feel pretty aggrieved, wouldn't you?

Why do you feel aggrieved? Because your property has been stolen? That you've worked hard for months to create your fruit and vegetables? That the newcomers have no right to them? If so, welcome to Nozick's world.

Nozick starts from the position that people have a moral right of ownership to themselves. You own yourself; I own myself. (Straightaway you can see that there's going to be a collision with utilitarianism in which your interests can be sacrificed for the greater good.) Having arrived on my island, as a distinct moral person with rights attached to me, I then use myself to change the nature of the island. Remember that I'm not taking the land from anybody, but what I am doing is to mix my labour with the land to create a product. Not only is the product mine (the strawberries, potatoes, etc.), but so is the land that I've now cultivated. It is now in a form that will make it easier to grow more crops. So you need to say to this lot who've come to your island and are stealing your crops: 'Go and cultivate your own piece of land as I did with this. Then that land will belong to you, just as this belongs to me.' You might, of course, choose to give these people some of your produce to help them on their way. But, as Nozick would stress, you are not required to.

Now bring yourself off the island and back to your present-day society. For Nozick, the context has changed but not the ethical theory. Each day, people go to work (mixing their labour with something to create a product or service). Each pay day, they are paid only part of what they earn. The rest goes in taxation. So each pay day, someone comes along and, in a Nozickean sense, steals some of your strawberries and potatoes. For Nozick, this is completely unacceptable. It means that you no longer own yourself. Your moral right to your self has been taken away. Kant's requirement that people should not be treated as means rather than ends has been violated.

So where does this position take us? State-supplied welfare becomes a form of slavery, in that it is paid for by requiring people to work for others. When UK university students protest loudly about having to pay fees, a Nozickean observer would see their protest as them saying, 'We are entitled to your money, whether or not you want to give it to us.'

There are various problems with Nozick's position. For one thing, it presents an oversimplified account of property rights. On our imaginary island, his theory seemed to work well. In a sophisticated modern economy, it is much more difficult to apply it. We are much more interconnected than the people on the island. To get from A to B, for example, requires me to expect that all sorts of people have co-operated to ensure that I can. A very good example of interconnectedness is that given in the essay 'I, Pencil: My Family Tree as Told to Leonard E. Read'.[11] This takes all the operations and materials (trees, steel-making, rope-making, graphite-mining and many others – including coffee growing needed for the workers at each stage of the process) involved in the production of a pencil and shows how its complexity requires significant co-operation.

There is also the problem of ownership. On my uninhabited island, I didn't have to worry about people already owning bits of it. But in a modern developed society, things have already been largely packaged up into people's existing property rights. In our example of the problem of pay differentials, we might need to look at the question of ownership. In what sense is the director of human resources more of an owner of the company's output than the secretaries or the juniors or the maintenance workers?

You can see that Nozick's position will have a lot to say about decision making, which requires us to distribute resources from one group to another. We will meet it again in this connection.

ISSUES OF DISTRIBUTION OF RESOURCES

Much decision making is indeed to do with how we should distribute resources. We met one such decision (a possible dilemma) when we looked at the problem of how to distribute a life-saving drug, and applied a utilitarian perspective to the problem. But there are other ways we can approach such problems.

Scarce resources can be distributed according to

- need;
- desert;
- right.

NEED

Need is a familiar criterion to use in deciding who should get what. It's often one of the principles used in the distribution of welfare resources in a country.

- Who should get priority for health care?
- Who should get financial help from the State?

These questions (and many more like them) could all be answered with the answer, 'Those who need it.' The sick and the poor would both come into the category of need.

As you will have noted very strongly, how need is defined is a question that requires an answer. It will normally be defined relative to the issue under consideration. Thus it could be defined in terms of income levels, housing conditions, medical conditions, educational performance and so on. It could also be a combination of these.

Obviously Nozick would have none of this. The fact that you need help has no necessary ethical significance for me. I might choose to respond but your need is more your problem than mine. The utilitarian might be interested in responding to need, but it would depend on the outcome of doing so. Would it be the most effective way of maximising preferences? Deontologists such as Rawls would be very sympathetic to looking at need. People in considerable need will find it very difficult to be autonomous and, anyway, what about the problem of justifying not responding to need from behind the veil of ignorance?

DESERT

Desert is a criterion that looks at the problem very differently. It asks the question, 'What people deserve to receive a resource?' Like need, it often comes up as an issue with welfare resources. Let's consider the same questions as before.

- Who should get priority for health care?
- Who should get financial help from the State?

The answers now are not the same. Who deserves to get priority for health care? Think of this question in relation to the smoking debate. The point has been made many times that those people who smoke do not deserve help when they are ill in the same way as those who don't. When the Northern Ireland footballer George Best was given a liver transplant, there was a debate as to whether, as a result of his very heavy drinking, he deserved to have one (as opposed to whether he needed one).

Who should get financial help from the State? Those who have not wasted money that they'd received? Those who would spend the money wisely? Those who've lived law-abiding lives? People who've given up their job might not immediately be entitled to help from the State. Why? Because it's seen that they don't deserve it.

RIGHT

The notion of 'right' is a response that is different again. Instead of looking at who needs a resource or who deserves it, we now consider who has a right to it. This is very often a simple case of who's entitled to help because of a legal entitlement. If you pay pension contributions over a minimum number of years, then you're entitled to draw that pension when the time comes. Even if you're a multi-millionaire or you've led a life of unbridled debauchery, you're entitled to your pension because you've entered into a contract which says you are.

Of course, a welfare system can draw on all of these criteria and most do indeed distribute resources on the basis of need, desert and right.

APPLYING NEED, DESERT AND RIGHT TO PAY DIFFERENTIALS

How relevant are these three concepts in our decision-making scenario of pay differentials?

An organisation that pays people according to need is one that we are largely unfamiliar with. But it is an interesting one. Our income pyramid would not necessarily have the top managers at the peak and the lower clerical and maintenance workers and such like at the bottom. The top category would now include those with the largest number of dependents; those at the base of the pay pyramid would now include those with no (or very few) dependents and those, for example, with low housing costs (such as those who have inherited property). You might know this system from the phrase popularised by Karl Marx: 'From each according to their ability; to each according to their needs.' The Critical Thinker wouldn't commend it because it has an interesting pedigree, but would look at it in terms of its contribution to effective functioning. No doubt you'll think further about it.

An organisation that paid people according to desert would have to establish first what features would be accepted as contributing to 'desert'. They might include effort, commitment, lack of clock-watching, flexibility, commitment to improving skills, willingness to help colleagues and so on. On this basis, the presently low-paid secretary could be paid significantly more than the presently highly paid head of department given his or her high scores on qualities such as these. Similarly, a presently low-paid secretary should be paid even less because of a lack of effort, commitment, frequent clock-watching, inflexibility, lack of commitment to improving skills, unwillingness to help colleagues and so on.

An organisation that pays according to right will be the familiar one. In the context of an organisation, 'right' will refer in large part to organisational rights. Banding of pay according to grades of work will detail the rights of all staff. These organisational rates will, of course, be supplemented (and, in part, informed) by legal rights from employment law. But the nature of the differentials will be in large part determined within the organisation.

These last two approaches can, as you will probably have noted, be used in combination. Thus an organisation is very likely to include an element of desert in addition to rights. The hard-working member of staff might well have additional income as a reward. (This is, of course, not the same as productivity bonuses in which payment is linked to output as a right.) Including need as a criterion for determining payment in a non-welfare context will, however, be rare.

APPLYING ETHICAL THEORIES TO THE SUBJECT OF FOREIGN AID

In Chapter 3, we spent some time looking at the issue of foreign aid. It will be useful to apply the ethical theories we've been looking at in this chapter to this issue. We'll look first at the conflict between the nature of the political regime and the extent of need. How would the three ethical theories we have looked at clarify our decision making in this conflict?

WHAT WOULD A UTILITARIAN HAVE TO SAY ABOUT THE CRITERION OF THE EXTENT OF NEED?

- A utilitarian is going to be particularly interested in how we see the extent of need. Do we mean 'How many people are in need?' or 'What is the extent of people's need?' or both? If there are lots of people at starvation level, then there could be considerable increases in well-being if this was relieved. If the percentage of those in need who are starving is very low, then the increases in well-being might not be so dramatically high.

- To the extent that there is need (however we define it), an increased satisfaction of these needs would increase previously needy people's preferences. This could be detailed in terms of less malnutrition, more education, better health, better accommodation and so on.

- To the extent that need (however we define it) has been reduced, those who have given for this purpose might feel greater well-being.

- Of course, the well-being of at least some of those who have given might decrease. This could be (looking ahead to Nozick) because they had no choice in the giving. If the need-reduction has been achieved by governments giving money (and other resources) paid for out of taxation, the libertarians will very likely have their well-being reduced. This would also apply if banks had cancelled debts, and then passed the cost of doing so on to their customers.

- The evidence of public opinion would be relevant in assessing the previous two points.

WHAT WOULD A DEONTOLOGIST HAVE TO SAY ABOUT THE CRITERION OF THE EXTENT OF NEED?

- If we take a Kantian position that we should value autonomy, then (as we have seen) we have a duty to ensure that people's autonomy is preserved. People in considerable need cannot have autonomy. In this way, since the extent of need can be seen as the extent of non-autonomy, this criterion has to be accepted.

- If we join Rawls behind the veil of ignorance, then any level of need that we would not tolerate has to be unacceptable. In this way, the extent of need is a very important criterion.

- If we use the difference principle of Rawls, then the extent of need remains of central concern. We have seen that this principle allows inequality as long as the most unequal benefit most from this arrangement. Thus the extent of need has to be on the agenda. Those who are the poorest in the world (in the most need) would have to benefit from the present distribution of global resources more than others for us not to put it as a very important criterion.

WHAT WOULD A LIBERTARIAN HAVE TO SAY ABOUT THE CRITERION OF THE EXTENT OF NEED?

- The criterion of the extent of need is always going to be a problem for the libertarian, if we are talking about the extent of other people's need. Nozick might hand over some of his resources to help to reduce the extent of need, but he is not required to take this criterion into account.

So far we have considered that the criterion of the extent of need would fit with both the utilitarian and the deontological positions, but would not fit well with the libertarian. What about the criterion of the nature of the political regime?

WHAT WOULD A UTILITARIAN HAVE TO SAY ABOUT THE CRITERION OF THE NATURE OF THE POLITICAL REGIME?

- The utilitarian would have to be concerned that, unless we take the nature of the regime into account, any potential increase in well-being from giving financial help might not be maximised.

- If it could be shown that much of the financial help would be siphoned off through corruption, then the utilitarian would want to consider the reduced well-being of those who have given the aid. Knowing that this money ends up lining the pockets of corrupt officials would lead to a reduction of well-being virtually all round. (The exception is obviously those who benefit from the corruption.)

WHAT WOULD A DEONTOLOGIST HAVE TO SAY ABOUT THE CRITERION OF THE NATURE OF THE REGIME?

- The deontologist has the same problem as the utilitarian with the nature of the regime. If the nature of the regime is such that it prevents assistance producing the desired result, then the autonomy that the Kantian is seeking will not result. In this way, the nature of the regime has a great significance to this position.

- Rawls will be seeking to produce justice. If the nature of the regime gets in the way of producing (something like) this, then the nature of the regime is of great significance in determining how we should act. Either from behind the veil of ignorance or using the difference principle, we find that the nature of the regime is relevant to the problem of how we should relieve poverty in developing countries.

WHAT WOULD A LIBERTARIAN HAVE TO SAY ABOUT THE CRITERION OF THE NATURE OF THE REGIME?

- The nature of the regime is also significant for the libertarian. At an important level, the libertarian will always find corrupt and repressive regimes unacceptable. They take what is not theirs to take. (Although, of course, they will find any government unacceptable because of this.) In this way, the libertarian will have to see the nature of the regime as of great significance to decisions in this area.

- The nature of the regime will take on a particular significance to the libertarian if the money to help reduce need has been given freely. If I give to help the poor in developing countries, then I will be ethically enraged if this gift is stolen by those to whom it was not given.

So what do the ethical theories tell us about using these two criteria together?

All three positions are going to see the nature of the regime as a criterion that has to be included in decision making. Until it is taken into account, then the criterion of the extent of need cannot be used fully. The utilitarian cannot seek to usefully increase well-being; the deontologist cannot usefully increase autonomy, or justify inequality; the libertarian cannot allow the theft of property.

Now let's look at the two criteria of cost and public opinion. How would the three theories help us to decide which was the more significant?

WHAT WOULD A UTILITARIAN HAVE TO SAY ABOUT THE CRITERIA OF COST AND PUBLIC OPINION?

- It is clear that a utilitarian cannot ignore public opinion. If a particular decision conflicted with public opinion, then it is likely to lead to a reduction in well-being.

- However, we need to consider what we mean by 'public opinion'. Do we include only that of people in the donor nations or do we also include that of people in countries that will receive aid? Do we have to look at how keenly opinions are held? If I don't really worry too much about making poverty history, but you care very much that we should give as much as we can, does this mean your well-being is more important than mine? And what about my Nozickean neighbour who cares just as deeply as you, but her position is that money should not be taken from her in order to help others?

- Cost comes into the utilitarian framework as an issue that demands our attention by asking us whether the price of foreign aid can be justified. The utilitarian would have to ask the general question, 'Does the spending of money on foreign aid achieve the greatest level of welfare?' Specific questions could emerge from this general one. For example, 'Could we spend the money in different ways that would maximise welfare?'

  The Commission for Africa asked for an extra $25 billion a year between 2008 and 2010. This seems to be a huge amount of money, but it amounts to only 0.08% of the 22 richest donor countries' GDP (if this is a relevant consideration). So, if GDP is a relevant consideration, could we argue that the extra $25 billion a year could easily be afforded without there being a noticeable reduction in welfare for rich countries, but a big increase in the welfare of people in poor countries?

WHAT WOULD A DEONTOLOGIST HAVE TO SAY ABOUT THE CRITERIA OF COST AND PUBLIC OPINION?

- Does an emphasis on the ethics of duty cut through the possible conflict between cost and public opinion? In an important way, yes. Our duty to help people be autonomous and to act justly is not constrained by public opinion. It is a duty that cannot be rejected because, say, 56% of the population aren't in favour of spending money to help. The cost could indeed be justified if what was spent led to less injustice (more autonomy). Of course, if the amount that was given meant that we couldn't satisfy the need to act justly in our own country, then there could be a problem. For example, if the government said to the people of a poor inner-city area, 'You can't have your new hospital that would undoubtedly save lives because we've given this money to fund a new factory in Zimbabwe', then the people in this area could protest.

WHAT WOULD A LIBERTARIAN HAVE TO SAY ABOUT THE CRITERIA OF COST AND PUBLIC OPINION?

The libertarian is on comfortable ground here. Of course you can't sacrifice public opinion on the altar of ethical duty to others. If foreign aid costs the public money, and they haven't specifically consented to paying for foreign aid, then we would have to look at public opinion. When a charity says that 'What you should give is just the equivalent of a cup of coffee a week', our Nozickean citizen reminds the charity, 'Yes, but it's my cup of coffee.'

So where have we got to with putting cost and public opinion together?

If spending whatever money is necessary leads to an overall increase in well-being, then the utilitarian will sleep easily in their bed tonight. If public opinion is not in support of spending this money, then they would have to stay awake fretting about a possible reduction in the public's well-being (depending, as we have seen, on how keenly this is felt, how many people feel like this, the improvements of welfare in poor countries and so on). Cost is therefore justified in terms of outcome.

For the deontologist, there is less of a problem to trouble their sleep. If public opinion is against helping the poor in developing countries, then there remains a duty to help (via Kant's emphasis on autonomy or Rawls' emphasis on acting according to principles of justice).

For the libertarian, if public opinion is against giving aid, then those who are against it cannot be ignored. Their opinion is central to the decision as to what to do.

In decision making about the distribution of welfare (as understood very generally to include pay differentials, public policies on health, transport, education and many other things), these three ethical positions will at the very least inform the decision-making process. The end-product – policy framework, decision, recommendation – might indeed be better for being informed in this way.

NOTES

1. A good example is N. Stewart, *Ethics*. Polity Press, 2008.
2. For a full account of the case, see R. Weis *Criminal Justice*. Hamish Hamilton, 1988.
3. See, for example, D. Ariely, *Predictably Irrational*. Harper Collins, 2009.
4. L. Chee Kong, 'A question of supply and demand', TODAYonline, 26 June 2010, www.todayonline.com/hotnews/EDC100626-0000100/A-question-of-supply-and-demand
5. T. Xuanwei, 'Death penalty, a trade-off', TODAYonline, 10 May 2010, www.todayonline.com/hotnews/EDC1000510-0000060/Death-penalty-a-trade-off
6. M. Gilbert, *The Holocaust: The Jewish Tragedy*. HarperCollins, 1989.
7. For example, see http://shass.mit.educ/research/philosophy
8. P.A. Fortes and E.L. Zoboli, 'A study on the ethics of microallocation of scarce resources in health care', *Journal of Medical Ethics*, August 2002, pp. 266–69.
9. J. Rawls, *A Theory of Justice*. Harvard University Press, 1971.
10. R. Nozick, *Anarchy, State, and Utopia*. Basic Books, 1977.
11. M. and R. Friedman, *Free to Choose*. Secker and Warburg, 1980. pp. 11–13.

6

LOOKING FOR STRENGTH
IN ARGUMENTS

We have looked at a wide range of issues to do with the process of inferences being drawn from claims. We have looked in particular at the form of an argument, the relationship between the reasons-side and the inference-side, the issue of relevance, and we have looked at decision making as a specific type of argumentation.

PERSUASIVENESS

The overall function of an argument is normally seen as to persuade those who hear or read it that it should be accepted. (It could be, of course, that the reader/listener is already persuaded, but they will probably enjoy having their position commended and reinforced.) This does not mean that a persuasive argument is necessarily a good one, in that people might be persuaded by one that should have little to commend it. (There are plenty of such examples in daily newspapers, especially those of a hysterical or preaching quality.)

PERSUASIVE NON-ARGUMENTS

Though the overall function of an argument is to persuade, this is not say that all persuasive presentations are arguments. We might be persuaded by poetry, drama, music, or paintings and photographs. Perhaps we can be persuaded that the reality of war is bad (as with Picasso's painting *Guernica*, Wilfred Owen's poem 'Dulce et Decorum Est' and Nick Ut's photograph of the nine-year-old girl running down a road in Vietnam after a napalm attack); perhaps we can be persuaded of the corrosive effect of jealousy by drama (Shakespeare's *Othello*); perhaps music can persuade us of the fickleness of love (Puccini's *Madam Butterfly*) and the delights of revenge against a former lover (Lily Allen's 'Smile').

Adverts have, of course, the central purpose of trying to persuade us to do something (normally to buy something). They might do this by simple reasoning, claiming various features for the product (effectiveness, low cost, attractiveness and so on) leading to a conclusion that one should therefore buy the product (including a specific recommendation not to buy a competitor's product). They might, of course, not make the conclusion explicit, leaving an inference to be drawn by the potential customer. There might not even be any specific claims, with everything being implicit (as with a series of images).

PERSUASIVENESS FROM LANGUAGE AND REASONING

MARTIN LUTHER KING

We could easily be persuaded by an account which isn't intended to be a well-constructed argument with its carefully worded reasons marshalled one-by-one leading to its conclusion. For example, if we read (or preferably listen to) Martin Luther King's 1963 'I have a dream' speech, we see that it is a powerful combination of historical claims, religious allusions, poetic language and political aspirations. However, at an important level, it is indeed an argument. The first part of the speech argues like this.

> (R1) Abraham Lincoln signed the Emancipation Proclamation in 1863 (a hundred years before).
> (R2) 'The Negro still is not free.'
> (R3) There is still discrimination.
> (R4) The Negro is still in poverty.
> (C) We've come to claim our rights.

This is a useful argument: the Emancipation Proclamation was very relevant to the problem of the continuing lack of civil rights, discrimination and consequent poverty of black Americans. King is appealing to consistency here (always a powerful appeal, if the appeal is to relevant aspects of the issue). If the Emancipation Proclamation promised freedom for slaves, then freedom for black people should be ensured. (The debate over the historical significance of the proclamation, however, makes the whole issue somewhat complicated.)

King uses a powerful analogy to support this argument. He argues that when 'the architects of our republic' wrote the Constitution and the Declaration of Independence, they 'were signing a promissory note to which every American was to fall heir'.

'It is obvious today that America has defaulted on this promissory note in so far as her citizens of colour are concerned. Instead of honouring this sacred obligation, America has given the Negro people a bad cheque; a cheque which has come back marked "insufficient funds". We refuse to believe that there are insufficient funds in the great vaults of opportunity of this nation. And so we've come to cash this cheque, a cheque that will give us upon demand the riches of freedom and the security of justice.'[1]

Analogies in arguments (like any other reasons-side argument-component) work only insofar as they are relevant to the content of the argument.[2] So you might wish to consider whether this analogy of a promissory note/bad cheque is a relevant one. More generally, is any law like a cheque that can be cashed? It's a very noteworthy analogy.

The speech has a considerable power, but it's a power that can't be reduced to the quality of the reasoning used. Much of the power comes from the language itself. Look at the next excerpt with some of the features of the language highlighted.

'Now is the time to make real the promises of democracy; now is the time to rise from the *dark* and desolate valley of segregation to the *sunlit* path of racial justice; now is the time to lift our nation from the *quicksands* of racial injustice to the *solid rock* of brotherhood; now is the time to make justice a reality for all God's children.'

This use of contrasting images is very powerful. The negatives ('dark...desolate...quicksands...injustice') contrast very strongly with the positives ('sunlit...justice...lift...solid rock...brotherhood...justice...all God's children'). Though we have seen that much of the power of the speech comes from there being an argument, perhaps the real power comes from the imagery and language used.

NEHRU

Another example of the powerful use of language in argumentation (specifically in this case, the use of metaphor) is the speech made by Jawaharlal Nehru after the assassination of Ghandi in 1948. He is speaking on the radio to tell the people of India of Ghandi's death.

'The light has gone out from our lives and there is darkness everywhere... Our beloved leader...is no more...The light has gone out, I said, and yet I was wrong. For the light that shone in this country was no ordinary light. The light that has illuminated this country for these many, many years will illumine this country for many more years, and a thousand years later that light will still be seen in this country...We must hold together, and all our petty troubles and difficulties and conflicts must be ended in the face of this great disaster.'[3]

Nehru argues that because of Ghandi's enduring 'light', the people of India must move forward and not engage in recriminations and revenge attacks. The speech has considerable power because of its use of language – 'the light', 'living, eternal truths reminding us of the right path', 'the living truth', 'taking this ancient country to freedom'. It's a good example of an argument having considerable power from the language that's used. But it also has a well-reasoned aspect, of which there are at least two examples. One is that, because Ghandi was against violence, people shouldn't engage in violence in revenge for his assassination. Another is that, because this was such a 'great disaster', all 'petty troubles and difficulties and conflicts must be ended'. The power of Nehru's speech thus comes from a combination of language and organisation.

Though we spent some time, especially in Chapters 2 and 3, on looking at issues with the use of language, we were concerned with the potential problems that a casual use of language can create. For example, the problem with the term 'future generations' was that it was often not clear which generations were included or excluded. However, King's use of the term 'the dark and desolate valley of segregation' is not to be treated as an example of over-casual use of language. Similarly Nehru's equivalence of Gandhi to a 'light' cannot be criticised in the same way that we might criticise a casual use of the term 'human rights'.

J.S. MILL

A particularly good example of a well-organised, well-delivered argument is that of J.S. Mill's 1867 speech to parliament in favour of women being given the vote. Here's part of it, a very strong appeal to consistency.

'We ought not to deny them [women] what we are conceding to everybody else – a right to be consulted; the ordinary chance of placing in the great Council of the nation a few organs of their sentiments – of having what every petty trade or profession has, a few members who feel specially called on to attend to their interests, and to point out how those interests are affected by the law, or by any proposed changes in it. No more is asked by this Motion.'[4]

This powerful appeal to consistency, such a strong requirement for a multi-reasoned argument, however, was unpersuasive. Women in the UK did not get the vote until 1918; it was not until 1928 that they got the vote on equal terms with men. This is a good example of the persuasiveness of an argument not being able to be reduced necessarily to its structure and content. In an important way, Mill was far ahead of his time. Though we might find his argument highly persuasive, its eventual success was not because the argument itself changed but the perception of it.

JOHN BALL

From a lengthy well-organised (but at the time unpersuasive) argument from J.S. Mill to a short but memorably persuasive two-lined rhyming argument in a question.

> 'When Adam delved and Eve span,
> Who was then the gentleman?'[5]

This powerful question is the beginning of a very short address made by John Ball, a clergyman who was part of what has become known as the Peasants' Revolt in 1381. The two-lined rhyming question is answered by Ball in a short but rousing speech. Here's a sizeable excerpt.

> 'From the beginning all men by nature were created alike, and our bondage or servitude came in by the unjust oppression of naughty men. For if God would have had any bondmen from the beginning, he would have appointed who should be bond and who free. And therefore I exhort you to consider that now the time is come, appointed to us by God, in which ye may (if ye will) cast off the yoke of bondage, and recover liberty.'[6]

What a well-argued case! In a very short argument we have a strong case against inequality. It hugely impressed the notable eighteenth-century politician and political thinker Edmund Burke, who praised the rhyming couplet at the beginning for its 'learning, sense, energy and comprehensiveness' and saw it as being 'fully equal to all the modern dissertations on the equality of mankind'. Burke added, however, that 'it has one advantage over them – that it is in rhyme.'[7]

Unfortunately John Ball's success in persuading people to rise up against inequality led to his capture and subsequent execution (being hanged and cut down whilst still alive, then disembowelled in front of the offended king, Richard II). Beware of the power of the rhyming couplet!

The use of metaphor to provide emphasis in argumentation continues to this day. In June 2010, in response to the massive oil spill caused by BP in the Gulf of Mexico, we have President Obama telling the American people that he had developed a 'battle plan' to combat the 'siege' in the Gulf and the oil that is 'assaulting our shores'.

RHETORIC

Aristotle was one of the great writers on the subject of rhetoric.[8] He saw this subject as having a very important role, not to be dismissed as some assessors of Critical Thinking do as 'mere rhetoric'. Would we dismiss Martin Luther King's 'I have a dream' speech as mostly 'mere rhetoric'? Would we dismiss John Ball's rhyming couplet in this way? Would we dismiss Nehru's sorrowful speech to the people of India in this way? Of course not (so it's a good job that King, Ball and Nehru weren't trying to get a qualification in Critical Thinking).

Aristotle was concerned to show that rhetoric was a combination of logic and philosophy. 'The tasks...of the orator are to find aspects of the subject that can be employed in arguments designed to establish the features that need to be stressed and that can be used to induce the appropriate emotional state in the listener and to create the impression of character.'[9] For Aristotle, the central task of the rhetorician is to provide the premises on which arguments are built, but he was also very much concerned with the relationship between the content of these arguments and the emotions. The dismissal of arguments as based on 'an appeal to emotion' would have been regarded as an oddity by Aristotle. The rhetorician, as the producer of effective arguments, is concerned not just with the nature of the premises but also on their effect in stimulating the emotions. Perhaps Critical Thinking needs to look at appeals to emotion with a more tolerant eye.

The role of rhetoric in persuasive argumentation is very often misunderstood. Here are two examples of this lack of understanding, both from the same source.[10]

> 'Rhetorical persuasion persuades through the use of words and emotive language rather than good reasons.'

The first oddity you'll have noticed is 'the use of words and emotive language'. What sort of words might these be, in addition to 'emotive language'? The second oddity is that rhetorical persuasion can and often does use 'good reasons' (Martin Luther King, etc.).

To compound these oddities, here's more from the same source.

> Rhetorical persuasion persuades us emotionally, and does not offer reasons which give strong support to the opinions it is trying to persuade us to agree with.

An example is given which the authors claim doesn't supply reasons, although this can be disputed. ('You can't be seen at the party in those. They're so yesterday. Whatever will people think?' As you can see, the second sentence is a perfectly acceptable reason for the inference in the first.) But the main thing to note is that 'rhetorical persuasion' that 'does not offer reasons' is not argumentation anyway. But what about rhetorical persuasion that does offer reasons? We could find plenty of examples of that.

These same authors then attack what they call 'rant', defined as 'giving opinions in a forceful manner [that] does not offer rational support for these opinions'. We're at a bit of a loss here: what's the meaning of 'forceful' and 'rational'? Does Martin Luther King's speech fall foul of this, with its forceful manner and use of metaphor: 'dark/sunlit', 'quicksand/solid rock'? Sorry, Dr Martin Luther King, that was no more than rant, so go away and write about emancipation of your people, omitting references to your having dreams and other such language.

FUNCTIONAL ANALYSIS OF ARGUMENTS

Though we are going to spend some time looking at the issue of function in argument, we need to remember that the persuasiveness of an argument (or even a non-argument) cannot always be captured through a functional analysis. An argument can have a notable complexity but be unconvincing; an argument can be simplicity itself and be highly persuasive. We should not forget that this whole issue of persuasiveness is a very big one. For example, Martin Luther King's speech presumably failed to persuade the members of the Ku Klux Klan of the need to honour Abraham Lincoln's 'promissory note'.

If the function of an argument is to persuade, then the function of each of the components of an argument should be seen as being intended to contribute to this intended persuasiveness. So, in looking at arguments, it is very useful to dismantle them into their components. Sometimes this functional analysis is very easy to do, in that an author has organised their reasoning in a way that is easy to follow. At other times, this is much harder, in that an author might deviate from their central line of argument or simply represent the same line of argument in different ways. Dismantling an argument is a bit like the work of a pathologist, as we dissect the structure of our argument lying before us. So, with our scalpel at the ready, what argument components are we looking for?

ARGUMENT COMPONENTS

- Any reasons
- Any intermediate conclusions
- A final (or main) conclusion
- Any evidence (including examples), used as support for reasoning
- Any counter-claims and/or counter-arguments
- Any 'scene-setting'
- Any explanations (not used as reasons)
- Any hypothetical reasoning
- Any analogies (and disanalogies)
- Any development/clarification of any the above

It is unlikely that we would find all of the above in any one argument. Arguments, as you know, can be sparse, especially syllogisms. But authors might well feel the need to spread themselves a little in their arguments. Let's look at an example and then unpack it.

EXAMPLE: CHANGES IN MASS TRANSPORT

Over the next 50 years, the availability of cheap oil is likely to decline significantly. This is because supplies of oil will decline and producers will increase the prices in order to compensate. Concerns about the way in which forms of travel seriously affect the environment are also likely to increase as these effects become more serious. In this situation, the way in which we travel could be changed significantly by 2060. Given that travel is central to our way of life, it would follow that our lives could be very different in 2060. There would be little long-distance travel for most people. Rural areas would become isolated again (as they were before the advent of mass travel). Most local transport would be by bicycle or even by horse. Most people would live close to where they work (with commuting being a very rare event). However, this scenario envisages there being no solution to the problems of the disappearance of cheap oil and the declining quality of the environment caused by mass transport. This cannot be the case. Clean alternatives to oil will be developed, such as hydrogen-powered vehicles, enabling us both to continue with mass transport and have a clean environment. We do not need to worry about the decline in the availability of cheap oil over the next 50 years.

EXAMPLE: CHANGES IN MASS TRANSPORT – FUNCTIONAL ANALYSIS

You will probably have spotted the main conclusion, conveniently at the end of the passage. But how did the author get there? Let's take the argument apart, section by section.

Over the next 50 years, the availability of cheap oil is likely to decline significantly. This is because supplies of oil will decline and producers will increase the prices in order to compensate.

This is an explanatory argument with the first sentence being, in an important sense, its conclusion, with 'supplies of oil will decline' and 'producers...compensate' being the reasons.

Concerns about the way in which forms of travel seriously affect the environment are also likely to increase as these effects become more serious. In this situation, the way in which we travel could be changed significantly by 2060.

The explanatory argument continues, with the first of the above sentences acting as a reason for the conclusion in the second (thus making the conclusion in the first section an intermediate conclusion). We can represent this explanatory argument in full.

(R1) Over the next 50 years, supplies of oil will decline.
(R2) Producers will increase the prices in order to compensate.
(IC) Over the next 50 years, the availability of cheap oil is likely to decline significantly.
(R3) Concerns about the way in which forms of travel seriously affect the environment are also likely to increase as these effects become more serious.
(C) In this situation, the way in which we travel could be changed significantly by 2060.

$$\frac{R1 + R2}{\downarrow}$$
$$\frac{IC + R3}{\downarrow}$$
$$C$$

This explanatory argument is then taken up in the next section. It's very much worth noting that the author's own argument has yet to start. All of this explanatory argumentation is going to have the function of a counter-argument.

> Given that travel is central to our way of life, it would follow that our lives could be very different in 2060. There would be little long-distance travel for most people. Rural areas would become isolated again (as they were before the advent of mass travel). Most local transport would be by bicycle or even by horse. Most people would live close to where they work (with commuting being a very rare event).

'Given that travel is central to our way of life' adds a reason to the previous conclusion from the explanatory argument to lead to the conclusion, 'it would follow that our lives could be very different in 2060.' What follows is detail of how different our lives could be.

If we add this section to the structure of the explanatory argument above, we get the following. (Note that the previous conclusion now becomes an intermediate conclusion, the fate of all inferences drawn on the way.)

(R1) Over the next 50 years, supplies of oil will decline.
(R2) Producers will increase the prices in order to compensate.
(IC1) Over the next 50 years, the availability of cheap oil is likely to decline significantly.
(R3) Concerns about the way in which forms of travel seriously affect the environment are also likely to increase as these effects become more serious.
(IC2) In this situation, the way in which we travel could be changed significantly by 2060.
(R4) Travel is central to our way of life
(C) It would follow that our lives could be very different in 2060.

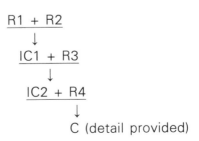

$$
\begin{array}{c}
\underline{R1 + R2} \\
\downarrow \\
\underline{IC1 + R3} \\
\downarrow \\
\underline{IC2 + R4} \\
\downarrow \\
C \text{ (detail provided)}
\end{array}
$$

However, this scenario envisages there being no solution to the problems of the disappearance of cheap oil and the declining quality of the environment caused by mass transport. This cannot be the case.

The author's own argument now begins (really the main point of the whole passage), in response to what is now seen as a counter-argument. 'However, this scenario envisages there being no solution to the problems of the disappearance of cheap oil and the declining quality of the environment caused by mass transport.' This presents in summary the problem with the previous position and the author then claims that 'This cannot be the case.' The author must then show why it cannot be.

Clean alternatives to oil will be developed, such as hydrogen-powered vehicles, enabling us both to continue with mass transport and have a clean environment.

A simple argument is presented.

(R) Clean alternatives to oil will be developed, such as hydrogen-powered vehicles, enabling us both to continue with mass transport and have a clean environment.

(C) It cannot be the case that there will be no solution to the problems of the disappearance of cheap oil and the declining quality of the environment caused by mass transport.

We do not need to worry about the decline in the availability of cheap oil over the next 50 years.

The main conclusion is thus drawn, with the previous conclusion now becoming an intermediate one.

(R) Clean alternatives to oil will be developed, such as hydrogen-powered vehicles, enabling us both to continue with mass transport and have a clean environment.

(IC) It cannot be the case that there will be no solution to the problems of the disappearance of cheap oil and the declining quality of the environment caused by mass transport.

(C) We do not need to worry about the decline in the availability of cheap oil over the next 50 years.

R
↓
IC
↓
C

The whole passage can be seen, then, as constituting two arguments, with the counter-argument being much bigger and more detailed. But it is the simple argument at the end which is the author's argument. It is interesting how the author has the curious way of appearing to lead us one way, only then to stop that line of argument with the word 'however'. This way of arguing can have some power. It sets up a position in order to show that there is an answer to it. In doing this, it is able to seek to show why the counter-position is, in the end, unconvincing. In terms of developing an argument for a position, it can be a useful approach in that one can see clearly (if the counter-position is accurately constructed) what one's own argument should address.

In the next argument, the author presents their argument in this way, by addressing issues that arise out of the counter-position.

EXAMPLE: MOBILE PHONES AND BRAIN TUMOURS

There has been a lot of public concern about the suggested link between mobile phones and brain tumours. However, not only is there an almost total lack of evidence showing any such risks, but more importantly there never could have been a plausible biological mechanism by which mobile phones could have caused brain tumours. If radio-frequency radiation caused brain tumours, we would have had evidence of this a long time ago from looking at radar operators who are exposed to large power levels. Quite simply, radio waves are incapable of damaging DNA. So why is it still believed that mobile phones could cause brain tumours? Part of the explanation is that the occasional study that shows a risk stands out against the vast majority that don't. In other words, they get noticed more than they should, even though there are questions that are often asked about their methodology and findings. In addition, studies that show no effect are very often not published because that's what we expect to find: they're not therefore seen as worth publishing.

It's sometimes pointed out that brain tumours have been increasing at the rate of 2–3% a year, so something must be causing the increase. There are two responses that can be made. In the first place, this increase has been going on for the past 30 years, so for much of the time long before mobile phones have been used widely. Secondly, as with many apparent increases in medical conditions, the change could be due to better diagnosis. The belief that there is a link between mobile phones and brain tumours needs to be rejected.

EXAMPLE: MOBILE PHONES AND BRAIN TUMOURS – DISMANTLING THE ARGUMENT

At this stage it is useful simply to isolate the parts of the passage. This can help to consider more clearly the function of each of the parts.

There has been a lot of public concern about the suggested link between mobile phones and brain tumours.

However, not only is there an almost total lack of evidence showing any such risks, but more importantly there never could have been a plausible biological mechanism by which mobile phones could have caused brain tumours.

If radio-frequency radiation caused brain tumours, we would have had evidence of this a long time ago from looking at radar operators who are exposed to large power levels.

Quite simply, radio waves are incapable of damaging DNA.

There never could have been a plausible biological mechanism by which mobile phones could have caused brain tumours.

So why is it still believed that they might?

Part of the explanation is that the occasional study that shows a risk stands out against the vast majority that don't. In other words, they get noticed more than they should, even though there are questions that are often asked about their methodology and findings.

In addition, studies that show no effect are very often not published because that's what we expect to find: they're not therefore seen as worth publishing.

It's sometimes pointed out that brain tumours have been increasing at the rate of 2–3% a year, so something must be causing the increase. There are two responses that can be made. In the first place, this increase has been going on for the past 30 years, so for much of the time long before mobile phones have been used widely. Secondly, as with many apparent increases in medical conditions, the change could be due to better diagnosis.

The belief that there is a link between mobile phones and brain tumours needs to be rejected.

EXAMPLE: MOBILE PHONES AND BRAIN TUMOURS – FUNCTIONAL ANALYSIS

The author starts with a little scene setting, which serves to give the thrust of the counter-position:

There has been a lot of public concern about the suggested link between mobile phones and brain tumours.

The word 'however', as before, signals that the author is going to respond to this counter-position. What follows provides two reasons, each of which directly supports the main conclusion.

However, not only is there an almost total lack of evidence showing any such risks, but more importantly there never could have been a plausible biological mechanism by which mobile phones could have caused brain tumours.

(R1) There is an almost total lack of evidence showing any such risks (of a link between mobile phones and brain tumours).

(R2) There never could have been a plausible biological mechanism by which mobile phones could have caused brain tumours.

Evidence (as a hypothetical claim) to support R1: If radio-frequency radiation caused brain tumours, we would have had evidence of this a long time ago from looking at radar operators who are exposed to large power levels.

Evidence-claim to support R2: Quite simply, radio waves are incapable of damaging DNA.

Question (re counter-position): So why is it still believed that they might?

The author's response to this question shows that they take the answer to the question to be, 'Because there are studies that show a link between mobile phones and brain tumours, and because brain tumours have increased.' The author then responds to this answer (though it is not explicitly given) with an 'explanation' in three parts, although this can be seen as an argument within the overall argument.

Part 1: The occasional study that shows a risk stands out against the vast majority that don't. In other words, they get noticed more than they should, even though there are questions that are often asked about their methodology and findings.

Part 2: In addition, studies that show no effect are very often not published because that's what we expect to find: they're not therefore seen as worth publishing.

These two parts of the explanation can be re-presented as:

(R1) The small minority that show a link between mobile phones and brain tumours are given undue attention because they are rare.

(R2) Studies that don't show a link are often not published because it is not expected that a link would be shown.

(C) (Therefore studies that show a link between mobile phones and brain tumours should not be seen as significant.) (This conclusion is implicit only.)

Part 3 is responded to by a separate argument.

Part 3: It's sometimes pointed out that brain tumours have been increasing at the rate of 2–3% a year, so something must be causing the increase.

There are two responses that can be made.

(R1) This increase has been going on for the past 30 years, so for much of the time long before mobile phones have been used widely.

(R2) As with many apparent increases in medical conditions, the change could be due to better diagnosis.

(C) (The increase in brain tumours cannot be shown to be caused by mobile phones.) (This conclusion is implicit only.)

Main conclusion: The belief that there is a link between mobile phones and brain tumours needs to be rejected.

Arguments like this one have two levels of structure. We can easily represent the main argument.

(R1) There is an almost total lack of evidence showing any such risks (of a link between mobile phones and brain tumours).

(R2) There never could have been a plausible biological mechanism by which mobile phones could have caused brain tumours.

Main conclusion: The belief that there is a link between mobile phones and brain tumours needs to be rejected.

$$\underline{R1 \ R2}$$
$$\downarrow$$
$$C$$

But, as we have seen, the author does much more than this. In particular the author deals with the counter-position in both an explicit and an implicit way. There are two sub-arguments that we have been able to identify. This is the first.

(R1) The small minority that show a link between mobile phones and brain tumours are given undue attention because they are rare.

(R2) Studies that don't show a link are often not published because it is not expected that a link would be shown.

(C) (Therefore studies that show a link between mobile phones and brain tumours should not be seen as significant.)

This is the second.

(R1) The increase in brain tumours has been going on for the past 30 years, so for much of the time long before mobile phones have been used widely.

(R2) As with many apparent increases in medical conditions, the change could be due to better diagnosis.

(C) (The increase in brain tumours cannot be shown to be caused by mobile phones.)

The relationship between these two sub-arguments and the main argument could be presented in the following way, to show their subsidiary status.

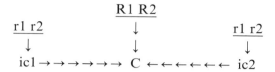

The power of this argument is in the way that it raises issues from the counter-position and systematically answers them (or, at least, you might want to say, sought to answer them).

This chapter began with the point that arguments are designed to be persuasive. We have seen that the persuasiveness of an argument can come from different sources. It can be from its simplicity (as with John Ball), its remarkable combination of rhetoric and organisation (as with Martin Luther King), its use of metaphor (as with Nehru), its wonderful relentless organised force (as with J.S. Mill), its careful identification and response to the counter-position (as with our last two passages).

The last two examples showed that careful functional analysis of an argument enables us to see much more clearly what's being argued. In doing this, we can, if we wish, move to evaluation of the argument. It brings us back to what we did in Chapters 2 and 3 on the value of clarity of language and what we did in Chapter 1 on structure and inference.

As a result, you can see that good argumentation comes in many different forms. Use rhetoric (when you need to); use careful organisation; use both. Produce simple arguments when they're appropriate; produce complex ones when they're necessary. You have now the potential to be a skilled, indeed a highly skilled, Critical Thinker.

NOTES

1. I. Pindar, *The Folio Book of Historic Speeches*. The Folio Society, p. 273.
2. See my *Critical Thinking for Students*. How To Books, 2010. pp. 83–8.
3. I. Pindar, *The Folio Book of Historic Speeches*. The Folio Society, p. 237.
4. I. Pindar, *The Folio Book of Historic Speeches*. The Folio Society, p. 154.
5. I. Pindar, *The Folio Book of Historic Speeches*. The Folio Society, p. 42.

6. I. Pindar, *The Folio Book of Historic Speeches*. The Folio Society, p. 43.

7. Quoted in R.B. Dobson, *The Peasants' Revolt of 1381*. American Council of Learned Societies, 2008. p. 394.

8. Aristotle, *The Art of Rhetoric*. Penguin Books, 1991.

9. H.C. Lawson-Tancred, 'Introduction' in Aristotle, *The Art of Rhetoric*. Penguin Books, 1991. p. 17.

10. J. Lally and C. Hart, A2 *Critical Thinking for OCR*. Harcourt Education, 2006. p. 5.

INDEX